TROUSERED APES

TROUSERED APES

DUNCAN WILLIAMS

With a Foreword by Malcolm Muggeridge

Arlington House
New Rochelle, N.Y.

For

Dominic, Rosamund and Christopher

CONTENTS

FOREWORD TO THE AMERICAN EDITION

I was particularly delighted to hear that there was to be an American edition of Professor Duncan Williams's brilliant book, *Trousered Apes,* and particularly honoured to be asked to provide the Foreword.

Here in England, the book began by being more or less bootlegged. Few reviewers noticed it (an honourable exception being C. P. Snow, who dealt with it at length), bookshops didn't stock it, the trade and the literary establishment left it severely alone. The reason is obvious. *Trousered Apes* (the title is taken from C. S. Lewis) is a cogently argued, highly intelligent and devastatingly effective anatomisation of what passes for culture today, showing that it is nihilistic in purpose, ethically and spiritually vacuous, and Gadarene in destination.

In the frenzied pursuit of novelty, in life as well as in art and literature, in the prevailing readiness to accept, and then almost at once reject, whatever is trendy, no matter how perverse or abnormal, Professor Williams sees the feverish attempts of a dying civilisation to clutch on to a swiftly ebbing tide. He follows Leslie Fiedler in detecting in the West today "a weariness with the striving to be men," the more desolating because, in this predicament, there is no turning to God, the news of whose death "has permeated, secularised and radically changed every aspect of Western thought and society."

Such a theme, presented with a great wealth of apposite illustration and force of argument, was bound to appall the servants of the conventional wisdom—the media pundits and situational clergymen, the crazed professors and lib ladies and Pulitzer prizemen and randy Catholic fathers, who dominate the literary, artistic and journalistic scene on both sides of the Atlantic, and who continue to propound the notion that change is progress, self-indulgence, liberation, and novelty, originality. Professor Williams's conclusion, to them anathema, is that we cannot live without God, and that when we try to we are fated, either to imagine ourselves to be gods and so able to shape our own destiny, flying like Icarus into the sun, or to relapse into carnality, seeking fulfilment through the senses. Resorting to sex, drugs and violence, and finding only satiety, fantasy and despair; succumbing, as what remains of Western civilisation so evidently is, to megalomania or erotomania, or both.

After the initial virtual boycott, little by little word began to get around that *Trousered Apes* had something very important to say, and said it uncommonly well. It was exactly like the circulation of subversive writings in the U.S.S.R. and other Communist countries; a mention here, a nod and a wink there, and the book began to move. It has gone on moving, with increasing momentum, ever since, without the slightest help from the *Times Literary Supplement*, the highbrow weeklies, the lowbrow dailies, advertising, media exposure, or any of the other means whereby publishers reckon to promote their authors and their wares. However, it finally achieved the distinction of being nominated Book of the Year in the London *Sunday Times*, *Sunday Telegraph* and *Observer*. The same thing, as I hope and believe, will now happen in America as discriminating, un-brainwashed minds get to hear that what Professor Williams has produced is no less than the theoretical, historico-philosophical justification for Tom Wolfe's splendid assault on Radical Chic.

I first heard of *Trousered Apes* from Christopher Booker, author of that climacteric book, *The Neo-philiacs,* which is very much in Professor Williams's vein. Thenceforth, I became part of the human chain passing it around, and in the process had the pleasure of meeting its author in person who turned out to be a very charming, erudite and intelligent academic. In a footnote in *Trousered Apes* he re-counts how he delivered a section of the book as a paper before a group of university teachers. When he had finished, a young lady of advanced liberal views came up to him and said in all seriousness: "You're advocating censorship; you shouldn't be allowed to publish it." She spoke truer than perhaps she knew, but after all the book *has* been published —just. How long this slender possibility of non-con-forming with the non-conformists survives will to a great extent depend on the degree to which the case Professor Williams so ably presents is understood and heeded.

Malcolm Muggeridge

June 1972

INTRODUCTION

To recognise the truth in a book is always a joyful thing. Again and again as I watched Professor Williams unfolding in this book the way that modern literature reflects the true cultural crisis of our times, I had that joy of recognition. And that is why I recommend his book with enthusiasm to all those who I know will enjoy it as much as I did.

I believe we are living just now in a very exhilarating time. That it is also deeply disturbing, frightening and confusing, goes without saying. But in the past few years, for at least a sizeable and growing minority, it has suddenly become much easier than ever before to grasp the true nature of our civilisation's predicament. For several hundred years we have, as a civilisation, been travelling along a certain road—accumulating along the way a whole lot of assumptions about where we were going which it has been very difficult to see through. We have all been conditioned to accept a certain view of progress. And now, quite suddenly, we are being emancipated from the vast deadweight of all those assumptions. We are finally face to face with the abyss to which that view of progress has led us: the prospect of a society not only threatened by nuclear war, by pollution, by over-population, but one in which men, depersonalised by their technology and their faith in science, have lost any sense of their own dignity or purpose.

The 16th-century historian Vasari observed that once human affairs begin to deteriorate, no improvement is possible until the nadir has been reached. In a way, the wakening up of many people today is due to their sense that a nadir has been reached. Professor Williams's excellent and readable book is part of this waking up process, and as such I hope it will reach a large number of people who are similarly waking up, and who will be strengthened by it.

The essence of his purpose is to show, through the mirror of modern literature—Dostoevsky, Camus, John Osborne, Jarry and a host of others, splendidly documented—what happens when men lose sight of the centre, as in Yeats's celebrated lines 'things fall apart, the centre cannot hold'. The 'trousered ape' of the title is the last, violent, neurotic hero who wanders through a thousand modern plays and novels, the 'anti-hero' of our civilisation. Since Rousseau two hundred years ago first glorified the 'noble savage', freed from all the restraints of civilised social behaviour, we have witnessed the gradual elevation into the centre of the literary stage of the ignoble savage—post-civilised, as opposed to pre-civilised, man; man increasingly bereft of a sense of purpose, of scales of value, of appreciation of order, harmony and morality—reduced ultimately and inevitably to nothing more than his basic animal instincts.

As Professor Williams shows, literature is not just an isolated thing, any more than the cinema, painting or any of the other arts. These are not merely diversions, but true mirrors of the preoccupations of the times, in which men not only find what they think amusing or important but also subconscious models for their own values and behaviour. When men cease to aspire to the ideal, the good, to self-restraint—whether in their arts or their lives—they do not just stand still, but actually turn the other way, finding self-fulfilment in self-indulgence, and in an obsession with those three ultimate expressions of the totally self-centred life: sex, violence and insanity.

Well, that is the road of which we have in a sense come to an end. In the arts at least, after the last ten years, there is hopefully little further in degradation and meaninglessness to be explored. And that is one reason why, if we are intellectually and morally honest, we are now able to look at the whole process of deterioration in some kind of perspective, and admit that the rot did not just set in with *Oh! Calcutta!* or *Waiting For Godot*, or even the 'shadow of the H-Bomb', but long before any of these things—when men ceased collectively to look upwards, and began to find significance only in the lowest common denominator of themselves.

When did this falling off first show itself? Here perhaps I would add my only qualification to Professor Williams's thesis, albeit one which follows agreement with almost every word he has written. Professor Williams seems to place his 'Golden Age', from which our present decline has taken place, in the classical ideals of the 18th century, in Pope, Dryden, Johnson, Jane Austen and other writers whom he quotes to great effect.

But can we place even the first seeds of the ultimate decay as recently as the Enlightenment? What is the real cause of the predicament of modern man which Professor Williams so brilliantly analyses? The ultimate answer, implicit in his text, must be that man has tried to stand on his own feet, to find his ultimate significance in the material world. Everything the Professor describes is what follows when men lose sight of their eternal significance, and of their dependence on God. And by a larger view, must we not agree that Western man has been collectively embarked on this adventure for longer than just the past two hundred years—certainly since, at the time of the Renaissance, it was once again proudly proclaimed that man could become 'the measure of all things'? Again and again Professor Williams quotes those men who along the way have diagnosed the true nature of the disease: Yeats's lines already quoted above, for one; and those from Pope's *Dunciad* which form the book's epigraph. Nevertheless there are at least two other quotations which would not have been out of place, both of which also sum up the growing disease of Western civilisation, even though they both come from much earlier than the 18th century. The first is Ulysees' famous speech from *Troilus and Cressida*—'take but degree away, untune that string, and mark what discord follows'; and the other, almost exactly contemporary, is from Donne's *First Anniversarie* describing how, when men lose the sense of God and virtue—'Be more than man, or thou art less than an ant' —then inevitably, by degrees, does 'the world's whole frame' fall 'out of joynt'; until finally it seems that the world becomes so sick that 'a Hectique fever hath got hold of the whole substance, not to be contrould'.

Again and again, not just today, but all through history, we come back to this same problem: that when man loses the centre, his life becomes meaningless, his world falls apart. It is true for individuals, it was true for the Roman world before us. But always the miracle remains—that, whatever happens to civilisation as a whole, even if it seems by its defiance of God to be quite doomed, for each individual the Centre and the Truth are still there, to give sense and purpose back to it all. And that is something from which 'neither death nor life, nor things present nor things to come' can ever separate us.

April 1971   *Christopher Booker*

AUTHOR'S PREFACE

This book has grown out of a paper delivered before a group of American university teachers of English in 1966. The ensuing discussion and controversy lasted well into the night and persuaded me that the subject demanded a more detailed examination.

Nothing that has happened since has changed my opinion that the Western World and its culture are saturated with violence and animalism. All who read newspapers or *avant-garde* novels or watch television news programmes can glimpse the truth of this statement, but few seem aware of its underlying causes.

To understand the true nature of the chronic upheaval which is engulfing our culture and, indeed, our entire civilisation, we must look into the past and attempt to trace its genesis there. My inquiry has led me to many unpleasant truths, and I regret that much of what I have written may prove unpalatable to colleagues and writers whom I would not wish to hurt or defame, but I believe society confronts a crisis which can be arrested only if we grasp its nature and dimensions in an honest manner.

I must not miss this opportunity of expressing heartfelt thanks to the following who encouraged me at various stages of bringing the original essay to this finished book: Lord Snow, Mr John Ciardi (Poetry Editor of the *Saturday Review*), Professor Walter Jackson Bate of Harvard University, and Professor Paul Schilpp of Southern Illinois University, Professor Shiv Kumar (chairman of the English Department at the University of Osmania, Hyderabad, India), Dr Jack R. Brown and Dr Howard A. Slaatte (chairmen, respectively, of the Departments of English and Philosophy at Marshall University). Even with such backing I could not have reached this stage without support from Mrs Pamela Kelsey, who uncomplainingly typed and re-typed the manuscript, and my wife whose patient understanding and encouragement made this book possible.

Finally, I must thank Christopher Booker for writing an eloquent introduction that recalls the outstanding sensitivity and insight of his *Neophiliacs*[1], which may yet prove a landmark in our return to a saner society.

Marshall University,   T.D.D.W.
USA
August 1970

[1] *The Neophiliacs,* a study of the revolution in English life in the fifties and sixties: published 1969 by William Collins and 1970 by Fontana Books.

TROUSERED APES

She comes! she comes! the sable throne behold
Of night primeval, and of chaos old!
Before her Fancy's gilded clouds decay,
And all its varying rainbows die away.
Wit shoots in vain its momentary fires,
The meteor drops, and in a flash expires . . .
Thus at her felt approach, and secret might
Art after Art goes out, and all is night.
See skulking Truth to her old cavern fled,
Mountains of casuistry heap'd o'er her head!
Philosophy, that lean'd on Heaven before,
Shrinks to her second cause, and is no more.
Physic of Metaphysic begs defence,
And Metaphysic calls for aid on Sense!
See Mystery to Mathematics fly!
In vain! they gaze, turn giddy, rave, and die.
Religion, blushing, veils her sacred fires,
And unawares Morality expires.
Nor public flame, nor private, dares to shine;
Nor human spark is left, nor glimpse divine!
Lo! Thy dread empire, Chaos! is restor'd
Light dies before thy uncreating word:
Thy hand, great Anarch! lets the curtain fall;
And universal Darkness buries all.

Alexander Pope: *The Dunciad,* Book iv.

1 The Ape Observed

Caliban casts out Ariel
Ezra Pound: 'Hugh Selwyn Mauberley'

In a Foreword to his book, *In Defense of Reason*, Yvor Winters observes that

'professors of literature, who for the most part are genteel but mediocre men, can make but a poor defence of their profession . . . and thus the study of one of the most pervasive and powerful influences on human life is traduced and neglected'.

While largely agreeing, I do not believe that Professor Winters is being entirely fair to his colleagues. The implication that all other humanists and scientists are exceptional men, eminently capable of defending *their* professions, passionately aware of the influence and impact of *their* studies and discoveries upon contemporary life, is difficult to accept, because there are comparatively few in any generation who are interested not merely in the humanities or sciences, but also in the fate of humanity itself. I would however agree that literature, in which I include the theatre, is indeed both pervasive and powerful and would add that most of us who teach it in colleges and universities are concerned to an alarming degree with trivia, as a scrutiny of recent articles in the learned journals in the United States and Europe would show.

Literary research has shared the fate of other disciplines and increasingly betrays an academic provincialism, the inevitable price of specialisation.[1] This makes it difficult for us to withdraw and observe the direction in which literature and literary criticism are moving. Fortunately, there are exceptions, one of whom was the late C. S. Lewis from whose book, *The Abolition of Man*, my somewhat esoteric title is taken. It is not without significance that Lewis wrote his book while at Oxford, a university which, in the words of a former Rhodes scholar, 'provides the last true luxury—time'. This is a luxury which fewer and fewer scholars now enjoy: I am referring not to time spent in serving on problem-shelving committees or in attending overcrowded academic conventions, but to an opportunity for thought and contemplation. 'Leisure', wrote Shaw, 'is the sphere of individual liberty; labour is the sphere of slavery.' Despite appearances, the academic community is being pressured in a variety of ways to involve itself in routine minutiae which make independent thought increasingly difficult. As a consequence, university teachers are in danger of an unthinking acceptance of prevailing ideas —a form of intellectual servitude.

What follows has been gestating in my mind for several years, but has lately, for reasons which I hope will become obvious, assumed an immediacy. Not only do I believe that literature is caught up in what Oswald Spengler aptly termed 'the great crisis of the present', but furthermore that it is to a remarkable degree responsible for this crisis. Nor should this surprise us. Literature is no longer regarded as a passive reflector, as a mere mirror which faithfully presents a picture of contemporary manners and morals; it is seen also as modifying the sensibility of the age, while at the same

[1] Marshall McLuhan's definition of a specialist is both provocative and pertinent: 'One who never makes small mistakes while moving towards the grand fallacy'.

time portraying it. As T. S. Eliot observed in his essay, 'Religion and Literature':

> 'When we read of human beings behaving in certain ways, with the approval of the author, who gives his benediction to this behaviour by his attitude toward the result of the behaviour arranged by himself, we can be influenced towards behaving in the same way'.

In the following pages I shall be concerned not so much with the artistic or aesthetic values of the works discussed as with their social and ethical impact upon our culture. This approach has one or two major pitfalls. It is comparatively easy to look back on previous historical epochs and note what Ortega y Gasset has called the amazingly compact unity which each presents through its various manifestations, and how identical the artistic and sociological trends are when viewed in this same perspective. When we turn to our own age, however, the vision becomes blurred, the trends seem to lack that compact unity, disparate forces appear to be at work. The complexities of modern life seem to preclude the possibility of any such clear view. I admit the difficulty, but do not regard it as insuperable. A number of logs floating on the surface of a river may point in apparently random directions; some will point down-stream, some horizontally to the banks, others at varying angles. The casual observer might regard them as being directionless pieces of timber, but a penetrating eye discerns that in spite of their divergent positions they are all being borne in one direction by the current. At times they move with great rapidity, at others the movement may be so slow as to be almost unobservable.

This phenomenon has a parallel in the *Zeitgeist*, that is in the intellectual and moral tendencies of an age. Beneath the surface there is a current, a predominating trend. The analogy may be carried a step further. It is when the river is flowing most swiftly that the logs, responding to the strong current, will exhibit the greatest uniformity of direction and the majority will point down-stream. Such was certainly true, for example, of the epoch which culminated in the French Revolution of 1789 and forced Edmund Burke, who had previously used his great ability and energy to combat what he regarded as the detestable doctrines of the revolutionaries in France, to the conclusion that

'if a great change is to be made in human affairs, the minds of men will be fitted to it; the general opinions and feelings will draw that way . . . and then, they who persist in opposing this mighty current in human affairs will appear rather to resist the decrees of Providence itself, than the mere designs of men'.

It is this current, this trend in contemporary literature and society which I am attempting to identify, and here lies another pitfall. Having defined what one believes to be this dominant trend, one must then recognise the danger of resembling Walter Shandy, who would 'twist and torture everything in nature to support his hypothesis'. My success in guarding against this temptation each reader will have to judge for himself.

Let us first of all examine two passages written by English authors, both dealing with a domestic situation and both involving a conversation between husbands and wives. In the first, the couple are discussing the possibilities of marrying off their daughters:

'Mr Bennet, how can you abuse your own children in such a way? You take delight in vexing me. You have no compassion on my poor nerves.'

'You mistake me, my dear. I have a high respect for your nerves. They are my old friends. I have heard you mention them with consideration these twenty years at least.'

'Ah! you do not know what I suffer.'

'But I hope you will get over it, and live to see many young men of four thousand a year come into the neighbourhood.'

'It will be no use to us if twenty such should come, since you will not visit them.'

> 'Depend upon it, my dear, that when there are twenty, I will visit them all.'

In the second passage the husband is analysing his sexual relationship with his wife:

> 'Oh, my dear wife, you've got so much to learn. I only hope you learn it one day. If only something—something would happen to you and wake you out of your beauty sleep. If you could have a child, and it would die. Let it grow, let a recognisable human face emerge from that little mass of india rubber and wrinkles. Please—if only I could watch you face that. I wonder if you might even become a recognisable human being yourself. But I doubt it. Do you know I have never known the great pleasure of love-making when I didn't desire it myself. Oh, it's not that she hasn't her own kind of passion. She has the passion of a python. She just devours me whole everytime, as if I were some over-large rabbit. That's me. The bulge around her navel—if you're wondering what it is—it's me. Me, buried alive down there, and going mad, smothered in that peaceful looking coil. Not a sound, not a flicker from her—she doesn't even rumble a little. You'd think that this indigestible mess would stir up some kind of tremor in those distended over-fed tripes—but not her! She'll go on sleeping and devouring until there's nothing left of me.'

The first extract is of course from the opening chapter of *Pride and Prejudice* by Jane Austen, whom David Cecil called the 'last exquisite blossom of the eighteenth century'. He goes on to observe that, for Jane Austen, 'to be completely satisfactory as a human being you need to be not only good and sensible, but also well-mannered and cultivated . . . . It is', he concludes, 'a civilised philosophy for civilised people.' The second extract is from *Look Back in Anger*, by John Osborne, first performed in London in 1956 and heralded as the beginning of the 'new wave' in the post-war British theatre. The lines quoted are spoken by Jimmy Porter, the proletarian anti-hero of the play, to his socially superior wife, Alison, and to his good-natured friend Cliff. I attended a performance of this play shortly after it opened and can still recall the reaction of the unprepared audience when Porter, discovering that Alison is pregnant by him, says quietly: 'I don't care if she's going to have a baby. I don't care if it has two heads.'

It is possible to draw certain general observations from these two extracts which I propose to examine not as pieces of literature, subject to the usual critical canons, but as representations of the social and moral climate in which they were written. I concede that Osborne's play is no longer the ultimate in modernity; it undoubtedly appears mild and old-fashioned when compared with the works of William Burroughs or Edward Albee or a host of other contemporary writers. My reasons for choosing it are that I wish to restrict the comparison to writers of one nation (although the dominant characteristics of Osborne's play manifest themselves in the works of a majority of modern American and European writers), to avoid extremes if possible, and offer a work which would exemplify a recognisable, dominant trend. (I should also like to stress that what follows is in no way an implied stricture on Mr Osborne's later plays.)

Most readers would agree that the overall impression that one gets from the conversation between Mr and Mrs Bennet is one of moderation and restraint; Mrs Bennet may indeed be as Jane Austen describes her, 'a woman of mean understanding, little information, and uncertain temper', but her husband regards her with amused tolerance and a *civilised* urbanity. In contrast, Jimmy Porter reveals a passionate and violent contempt for his wife and the whole upper-class world which she represents, the world of the country-gentry. When I recently re-read the play, I was reminded of a passage in Spengler's *Decline of the West*, in which he anticipated the advent of Jimmy Porter and his kind:

'In place of a type-true people, born of and grown on the soil, there is a new sort of nomad, cohering unstably in fluid masses, the parasitical city-dweller, traditionless, utterly matter-of-fact, religionless, clever, unfruitful, deeply contemptuous of the countryman and especially that highest form of countryman, the country-gentleman.'

In addition to the contempt Porter exhibits towards his wife, a contempt expressed as the title of the play suggests in *violent*, angry outbursts, there is an *animalism* quite obviously present in the excerpt. Alison has 'the passion of a python'; every time they have intercourse he is devoured like 'some over-large rabbit'. Here, I suggest, are the two dominant themes of modern literature and drama, the manifestations of the *Zeitgeist* which we are seeking.

This conjunction of violence and animalism is found to a greater or lesser degree in almost every recent best-seller or theatrical success from Edward Albee's *Who's Afraid of Virginia Woolf?* to Truman Capote's *In Cold Blood*, from Peter Weiss's *Marat-Sade* to John Barth's *Giles Goat-Boy*. There was a certain savage irony in the fact that, while one of the worst race riots was taking place in the United States, several local cinemas were showing a film entitled *Devil's Angels*, with the accompanying advertisement: 'Violence is their God! and they hunt in a pack like rabid dogs.' We shall later examine the effects of such 'entertainment' on the contemporary mind. Suffice it, at present, to remark that we are teaching savagery and are naively appalled at the success of our instruction. It is perhaps more than coincidental that when Martin Luther King was assassinated, *Bonnie and Clyde*, a film glorifying two perverted killers, was among those nominated for an Academy award. As Pamela Hansford Johnson has warned in her powerful book, *On Iniquity*, 'The flood of sadistic pornography which is making the western

29

world look so hideous . . . is conducive to a madness of our whole society.' It is, moreover, no longer confined to the semi-literate, luridly-covered and easily recognisable variety but has become the dominant *motif* of the modish, contemporary, intellectual climate.

This anti-civilising trend has been remarked upon by a number of critics and writers. For example, Lionel Trilling, in *Beyond Culture* has stated that 'the characteristic element of modern literature, or at least of the most highly developed modern literature, is the bitter line of hostility to civilisation which runs through it'; while the novelist, Norman Mailer, openly acknowledges that 'whether the life is criminal or not, the decision is to encourage the psychopath in oneself'.[1] Writing of Bŭnuel, the Spanish film-director who specialises in portraying the sado/masochistic mentality, Henry Miller observes: 'Either you are crazy, like the rest of civilised humanity, or you are sane and healthy like Bŭnuel. And if you are sane and healthy you are an anarchist and throw bombs'. Few, however, seem to recognise in this trend anything more than a purely literary or artistic phenomenon. It appears to be forgotten or ignored that literature and the arts in general are very real, formative, social forces, moulding the face of the age while at the same time portraying it.

Returning to Osborne's play, it would be foolish to assert that Jimmy Porter embodies either of the two qualities—violence and animalism—to any advanced extent, or that *Look Back in Anger* is an example of

---

[1] Ernst Jünger, the German philosopher, reached a similar conclusion to Mailer: that it is better to be criminal than bourgeois. Sartre, also, appears to lend support to this doctrine, when he canonises Genet, a self-confessed pervert and thief. To equate the saint and the criminal, because both lead an existence outside normal society, would seem to be as illogical as to equate white and black on the grounds that neither is a neutral colour.

sadistic pornography. At the same time, Porter is useful in that he is a recognisable modern literary and social phenomenon. His descendants are visible, nightly, on countless millions of television screens; they can be seen parading their arrogant primitivism on the stage, appearing with calculable regularity in the pages of currently fashionable fiction. He, himself, epitomises the trousered ape of my title and as such merits attention. To observe him is unavoidable; to understand him requires that we look into the past to trace his genesis; to assess his importance and affectiveness, in sociological as well as literary terms, it is necessary to speculate upon the nature and destiny of man. What follows is an attempt to encompass these objectives.

2 Man and Brute

'It requires a pretty deal of pains to distinguish ourselves from brutes. We must have a share of probity, honour, gratitude, good sense, and a complacency for our species in general to render us worthy of that name, so that all who are designed for men are not rightly called so till acquired advantages confirm their title.'

Mrs Mary Davys: *The Accomplished Rake* (1727)

Western man, from pre-Socratic times, has recognised the essential dualism of his nature, but the combined forces of Christianity and classicism, utilising what one may term moral absolutism, stressed the importance of the spiritual and frowned upon the sensual and animalistic. Thus, St Paul in his Epistle to the Philippians urges them to let their thoughts run upon

'Whatsoever things are true, whatsoever things are elevated, whatsoever things are just, whatsoever things are pure'.

In the treatise *On The Sublime*, attributed possibly erroneously to Longinus but certainly the work of an author deeply imbued with classical thought, we find the following:

'Nature has appointed us men to be no base or ignoble animals; but when she ushers us into life and into the vast universe . . . forthwith she implants in our souls the unconquerable love of whatever is elevated and more divine than we'.

Finally, Dante, who can be regarded as a classical, Christian humanist, unites these two major trends in Western thought, observing in *De Vulgari Eloquentia* (written at the beginning of the 14th century) :

> 'that as man has been endowed with a threefold life, namely, vegetable, animal, and rational, he journeys along a threefold road ; for in so far as he is vegetable he seeks for what is useful, wherein he is of like nature with the plants ; in so far as he is animal he seeks for that which is pleasurable, wherein he is of like nature with the brutes ; in so far as he is rational he seeks for what is right—and in this he stands alone, or is a partaker of the nature of the angels'.

These three quotations embody the fundamental beliefs on which Western civilisation has been built, and it was not until the latter half of the 18th century, following upon and hastening the decline of neo-classical thought, that they were seriously questioned as a basis for morals and ethics. During the past two centuries, however, with spasmodic and ever-weakening reactions, these beliefs have been eroded until today there are few educated persons under the age of thirty who would not rather substitute for them William Blake's aphorism, 'Sooner murder an infant in its cradle than nurse unacted desires'. (One contemporary playwright, Edward Bond, appears to have taken this quite literally in his play, *Saved* (1965), in which a baby is stoned to death in its perambulator by some youths.)

The 20th-century interest in Blake is an identifiable manifestation of our epoch, the dominant trend of which has been an almost total rejection of the old moral sanctions in a search for 'self-fulfilment', or, as George Santayana has stated, 'a many-sided insurrection of the unregenerate natural man . . . against the regimen of Christendom'. Thus in 1926 we find the critic, I. A. Richards, writing in *Science and Poetry:*

> 'People who are always winning victories over themselves might equally well be described as always enslaving themselves. Their lives become unnecessarily narrow. *The minds of many saints have been like wells; they should have been like lakes, or like the sea*'. (Italics mine.)

33

Later in the same work, he defines an evil experience as 'one which is self-thwarting or conducive to stultifying conflicts'. T. S. Eliot carried this idea a stage further in his praise of Baudelaire in 1930 when he wrote: 'It is better, in a paradoxical way, to do evil than to do nothing: at least we exist.' This is, of course, simply a restatement of Blake's 'Active Evil is better than Passive Good', but it is also a dominant theme in *The Waste Land*, undoubtedly the most influential poem of this century, although it is significant that the views of the older Eliot differ markedly from the foregoing, which also explains their comparative lack of popularity. The Eliot of *The Waste Land* resembles a sea-captain who, having scuttled his ship, rows off in a small life-boat named Anglo-Catholicism and leaves the vast majority of his crew and passengers drowning. The extraordinary thing is that they appear to have enjoyed the experience; they enjoyed being told that they were living in 'rats' alley', and settled back to luxuriate in their social and religious ruins.

There is a cult of despair today and any optimism is regarded as sentimental drivel or worse. Trilling, in *Beyond Culture*, to which I have already referred, says that the

> imagination of felicity is difficult for us to exercise. We feel that it is a betrayal of our awareness of our world of pain, that it is politically inappropriate'.

He proceeds to draw attention to the 'psychic fact' that more and more of our authors (and presumably their readers) 'repudiate pleasure and seek gratification in—to use Freud's word—unpleasure'. This last remark would have appeared arrant nonsense to Samuel Johnson, who declared that 'the only end of writing is to enable the reader better to enjoy life or better to endure it'.

This cult of 'unpleasure' might seem to have no

connection with the violence and animalism which are the predominant characteristics of modern literature; but, if we examine this phenomenon a little more closely, we shall see that it is yet another integral part of the compact unity of our age. Violence is almost invariably the result of a sadistic impulse; the cult of unpleasure is simply another term for masochism. One does not need to be a psychologist to recognise in both these impulses the same desire to *hurt*.[1] They are, in fact, two sides of the same coin and equally repugnant to the classical ideal of civilised man, an ideal based upon serenity (or inner harmony), dignity, and restraint. To the extent that modern artists and writers lack this inner harmony, their products might be termed 'neurotic', were it not that all such normative judgements seem nowadays to be taboo.

This modern trend away from the old moral sanctions (an external morality) towards self-fulfilment can be observed in theology, philosophy and other disciplines, as well as in literature. Thus the 'New Morality' of the former Bishop of Woolwich, John Robinson, and *Situation Ethics* by Joseph Fletcher both revolve around this tendency, as indeed do the philosophical tenets of Christian existentialism. Basically, I have no quarrel with such views which uphold the substitution of individual (i.e. internal) standards for the old-fashioned, legalistic and external ones. There is, however, a very real danger in the *popularisation* of such ideas. Self-fulfilment demands a certain measure of restraint, of self-control. This is an adult concept, as I think even its exponents would agree, and in between these two

[1] Erich Fromm recognises the persistent conjunction of these two in certain personalities; both tendencies, he suggests, are the outcome of 'an inability to bear the isolation and weakness of one's own self'. (*Escape From Freedom.*)

plateaux, the old morality and the new self-fulfilment (or 'self-actualisation'), there exists a chasm into which, while attempting to cross, the majority falls. This chasm is self-indulgence, a descent to mere animal gratification, which presents the greatest danger to the immature who, vaguely aware of the demise of the old sanctions, delight in the permissiveness which increasingly pervades our society. The paper-back revolution, coinciding with concepts expounded by and intended for spiritually and morally adult minds, brings to a growing youthful majority a distorted message—instant gratification of all appetites with no bill to pay. This is not the intention of those who formulate these concepts but the inevitable result of an egalitarian society in which *everything* must be made available at all times to everyone. The dangerous consequences of this attitude will be more fully dealt with in a subsequent chapter.

The neo-classicists of the first half of the 18th century were well aware of the narrow margin which separates man from the brutes. Swift's Yahoos were a terrible object-lesson in what could happen to man if he were to forsake reason and abandon himself to his passions. Throughout this period, poets, novelists, philosophers, and theologians impressed upon society the need for restraint and self-control. Samuel Johnson expressed clearly and concisely the attitude of his age to the passions when he observed : 'Whatever withdraws us from the power of our senses . . . advances us in the dignity of thinking beings'.

I suspect that the average modern, regardless of his cultural or social background, would regard all such ideas as 'stuffy' or 'pompous', and, in his temporal provincialism, ridicule them. Yet a shrewd observer, F. R. Leavis, has pointed out that the insistence on good form, which characterised that age, was more than merely a social facade:

> 'With Dryden begins the period of English literature when form is associated with Good Form, and when, strange as it may seem to us, Good Form could be a serious preoccupation for the intelligent because it meant not mere conformity to a code of manners but a cultivated sensitiveness to the finest art and thought of the time. . . . Politeness was not merely superficial ; it was the service of a culture and a civilisation, and the substance and solid bases were so undeniably there that there was no need to discuss them or to ask what was meant by "Sense".' (*Revaluation,* 1964.)

It is worth pausing to examine exactly what were these fundamental beliefs of neo-classicism to which Leavis refers. Broadly speaking, there was a widespread feeling that man had at last reached a state of civilised existence, or at least was thought *capable* of leading such an existence. Poets and artists, philosophers and theologians prized clarity, ease, and balance and looked back in horror to what the historian Edward Gibbon called 'the dark age of false and barbarous science'. The diamond had been found and all that remained was to polish it until it reached a stage of near-perfection. Philosophically and theologically the educated and the cultivated leaned towards deism, which, with its emphasis upon a reasoned approach to religion and a corresponding lack of interest and belief in the more supernatural elements of Christianity, seems in retrospect so inevitably suited to the age. Above all, man saw himself as a being *in harmony* with the universe, which in turn was seen as the outward manifestation of the mind of the Creator. As Alexander Pope expressed it:

> All are but parts of one stupendous whole,
> Whose body Nature is, and God the soul.

It was by modern standards a comfortable, cosmic view which posed the question of how man could best

37

attain a state approaching the perfection of the universal order which surrounded him. It was to this moral question that the leading minds of the age addressed themselves and, to a surprising extent, a consensus emerged as to what constituted this ideal. Nor should we smile condescendingly on such a search. Hegel has remarked that the 'highest point in the development of a people' is reached when 'they have reduced its laws, its ideas of justice and morality to a science'. One might add that a strong culture invariably manifests a widespread belief in the validity of its basic norms; the converse is also true.

The ideal of neo-classicism has been well expressed by Walter Jackson Bate in *From Classic to Romantic*, when he talks of 'decorum' as 'the simultaneous preservation and ennobling of the type'. He also points to the essential contrast between the neo-classical outlook and the naturalistic:

'The more extreme naturalist may be said . . . to assume the lowest as the norm, and to view whatever is better as an unexpected gain . . . while the classicist conceives the highest as the norm and regards whatever falls below not as "natural" but as corruption'.

Traces of this classical outlook recur in the 19th century; Matthew Arnold, for example, maintained that 'culture . . . shows its single-minded love of perfection, its desire simply to make reason and the will of God prevail'.

If we apply Bate's statement to the two extracts from Jane Austen and John Osborne which we examined briefly in the last chapter, it can easily be seen into which category each will fall. Jane Austen would regard Jimmy Porter as a slovenly vulgarian, as 'abnormal', because he would appear to her refined and civilised mind as a latter day Yahoo; whereas Osborne would regard Mr Bennet as a representative of the hateful country-gentry, the embodiment of affectation and repression, and therefore of abnormality. In one important respect, however, most modern writers differ from Bate's naturalists by regarding anything better than the norm with suspicion and hostility, as a relic of the past, as a civilising influence to be hunted down and destroyed.

This is partly due to the temporal provincialism of the 20th century, which stems from an ignorant self-sufficiency; to a much greater extent, however, it originates in a cultural and social inferiority complex, never acknowledged and scarcely recognised even by those who manifest it most markedly. Again, Jimmy Porter is a revealing example exhibiting precisely this same inferiority complex in his relationship with Alison as do the majority of contemporary writers and artists in relation to Western culture.

Surprisingly, support for this statement has been supplied by Pablo Picasso. In a 'confession'* published in the French periodical *Le Spectacle du Monde* (November 1962), Picasso, after admitting that when young he was enamoured of 'the religion of great art', goes on to observe that as he grew older he perceived that art, 'as it had been conceived up to the end of 1800', had become sterile and moribund. Deploring the fact that his contemporaries have given their hearts to materialism—'the machine, scientific discoveries, wealth, the domination of natural forces and the things of this world'—he asks the question: 'Why then do the artists of today persist in sculpting and painting?' His answer is that they do so out of habit, out of ostentation, a love of luxury and for 'what they can get out of it' ('*par calcul*'). Admitting that 'from cubism on', he himself has satisfied the public with the 'many bizarre notions which have come into my head' and adding that 'the

* Note to the American edition: I have since found that the Picasso 'confession' is spurious. D. W.

less they [the public] understood, the more they admired them', he concludes as follows:

> 'Today, as you know, I am famous and very rich. But when I am alone with myself, I haven't the courage to consider myself an artist, in the great and ancient sense of that word. . . . I am only a public entertainer, who understands his age'.

The defeatism implicit in this bitter confession is not confined to painting. The whole modern cult of violence and animalism is in essence an admission of defeat. Since we cannot be men to any idealistic extent, let us lapse into barbaric animalism but, still clinging to vestiges of a past which we hate but cannot escape, let us clothe our defeat in high-sounding terms: 'alienation', 'cult of unpleasure', 'realism', and similar jargon. Yet all this fashionable phraseology cannot conceal the fact that the Emperor has no clothes. The literature of today lacks certain essential qualities. It no longer satisfies man's need for beauty, order, and elevation, and to this extent it is incomplete and stunted. It contains, as Trilling has observed, an anti-civilising trend, and to this is closely linked a cult of ugliness, a morbid concentration on the baser elements of life, a clinical obsession with the bizarre, with the grossly sensual and degrading aspects of human nature.[1]

---

[1] In July 1967, Picasso's play *Le Désir Attrapé par la Queue*, was given its first public performance on the outskirts of St Tropez. In a much-publicised scene, a female character, 'Tart', squats in the middle of the stage in a urinating position while a sound track makes appropriate noises. I must admit that the symbolism of this particular scene escapes me, but once again, the emphasis is unmistakable. The producer of the play, Jean-Jacques Lebel, is quoted as saying, 'We're not at liberty to emasculate a work of art to pander to bourgeois sentiment . . . The fact that there is so much opposition to the kind of thing we're doing is what gives us faith that we're on the right road.' One can only conclude that M. Lebel has never read Pope's lines:

> So much they scorn the crowd that if the throng
> By chance go right, they purposely go wrong.

This total rejection of tradition and of traditional morality and religion was foreseen by Spengler and denoted, in his opinion, the death-throes of a culture. He anticipated the modern megalopolis, which he termed 'the world-city', and observed that

'to the world-city belong not a folk but a mob. Its uncomprehending hostility to all the traditions representative of the Culture (nobility, church, privileges, dynasties, conventions in art, and limits of knowledge in science), the keen and cold intelligence that confounds the wisdom of the Peasant, the new-fashioned naturalism that in relation to all matters of sex and society goes back to quite primitive instincts and conditions . . . all these things betoken the definite closing down of the Culture and the opening of a quite new phase of human existence, anti-provincial, late, futureless, but quite inevitable'.

This brilliant analysis of contemporary society was written in 1917 ; and the only element in it with which I shall disagree is his belief in the inevitability of the cycle.

Certainly, if we accept his theory that a culture moves through successive stages—spring, summer, autumn and winter—then who can seriously doubt that what we are witnessing today is the death of a culture and of a civilisation ? The frenzied attempts to create a new art-form every month, the compulsive hunt for novelty (not only in the arts but in almost every sphere of human activity), the almost simultaneous acceptance and rejection of the latest, most modish, experiment however perverse or abnormal it may be—all these are symptomatic of a dying man's feverish attempts to clutch on to a swiftly ebbing life.

Modern writers mostly resemble a man who has inherited a magnificent, richly furnished mansion but out of ignorance or perversity proceeds to demolish it brick by brick and to throw the furniture away. Winter has come and he bemoans his lack of shelter and warmth. It may be recalled that in the novel *Charley Is*

41

My Darling a group of children systematically wrecks a house. The author, Joyce Cary, in his preparatory essay, after remarking that in real life such raids are not at all uncommon, goes on to observe that they are frequently caused by rage—'a rage against beauty and dignity by those who have neither but feel the want'. This would appear to lend support to my previous statement that many contemporary writers are subconsciously motivated by a similar feeling of inferiority in their relationship with the beauty and dignity of the past, resulting in an urge to destroy what they can neither surpass nor emulate.

It is surely significant that Allen Ginsberg, one of the most influential poets among contemporary youth, entitled his first collected volume *Howl*; that Evelyn Waugh, the most gifted of British satirists, named the last novel which he wrote *Unconditional Surrender*; and that the American poet, Robinson Jeffers, once described civilisation 'as a transient sickness'. The epigrammatic quality of this last remark should not blind one to its essential silliness; civilisation is nothing more than the restraining influence which prevents man from lapsing into barbarism, from descending to the level of the Yahoo, and no amount of persuasive casuistry or facile meliorism should blind one to this fact.[1] It would be interesting to know what alternative to civilisation Jeffers could provide.

Were this feeling confined to an ineffectual if vociferous minority, it would not matter overmuch, but

---

[1] The necessity for writing the above so soon after the bestialities of the Nazi concentration camps have been revealed, is proof (if such is needed) of the temporal provincialism of our age. Already the new advocates of the perfectibility of man through anarchy are raising their voices and demanding freedom from the irksome restrictions of civilised society.

it is surely time to acknowledge the danger signals when a critic of Leslie Fiedler's perspicacity sees

> 'a weariness in the West which undercuts the struggle between socialism and capitalism, democracy and autocracy; a weariness with humanism itself which underlines all the movements of our world, a weariness with the striving to be men'.

After all, as Karl Jaspers has expressed it in *Existenzphilosophie*: 'To fail to be human would mean to slip into nothingness'. William Golding's *Lord of the Flies* reinforces this warning. In one respect, however, Golding's book distorts the picture; there is no naval officer to rescue us from the onslaught of savagery. The news of His (God's) death has permeated, secularised and radically changed every aspect of Western thought and society. The tragic consequences of this awareness are implicit throughout the remainder of this book.

3 The Genesis of the Anti-Hero

Can aught exult in its deformity?
Shelley: *Prometheus Unbound*

Hegel maintained that the whole history of man is an ever continuing cycle of thesis and antithesis; we think we are progressing when in fact we are merely moving like a pendulum from one extreme to the other. The only two epochs when man achieved a state of synthesis would appear to be classical Greece and 18th-century Europe, particularly England. In both, man saw himself as a being in harmony with the universe and with society, which he regarded as a microcosm of that universe. If we regard Aristotle's *Poetics* and *Ethics* and Pope's *Essay On Criticism* and *Essay on Man* as establishing aesthetic and ethical theories for their respective ages, then this statement would appear to be broadly true.

In both periods society as a whole consciously aimed at attaining perfection, not only in architecture, music, poetry and other art forms, but also in the moral sphere. Thomas Aquinas saw the universe

'as a general sacrament . . ., [as a] principle of the ideal which the artist tries to reproduce, supreme end of all that was, is and will be, sovereign rule of all that we should do',

and one feels that the Greek classicist and the Augustan

neo-classicist would both subscribe to this view. Such epochs of synthesis however appear to carry the seeds of self-destruction within them; and beneath the apparently placid calm of the 18th century forces were at work in the last two decades which were to tear down most of the remaining walls of classical restraint.

Broadly speaking, the revolution took place in three major fields—politics, religion, and literature. Politically, the French Revolution brought to an end the *ancien régime* and caused Burke, in a well-known passage from his *Reflections on the Revolution in France*, to lament that

> 'the age of chivalry is gone—that of sophisters, economists, and calculators has succeeded; and the glory of Europe is extinguished forever'.

In religion, the preachings of John Wesley helped undermine the authority of the established Church of England. In the literary world a movement, the roots of which extended far back into the century and which was certainly not confined to any one country, came into full maturity. For want of a better name, I shall call this last 'romanticism' although, as Professors Lovejoy and C. S. Lewis have shown, this term has been so over-used that it has been rendered almost meaningless.

These three seemingly unconnected revolutions, on closer inspection, reveal that 'compact' unity of their epoch characterised by a rejection of authority and by an emotional appeal. The anti-authoritarian nature of the French Revolution is too apparent to need any comment. Wesley rejected the classical formalism of the church and his followers felt the need to establish themselves as a separate body. 'Romanticism' was largely a powerful reaction to the restraint and moderation of neo-classicism. (James Joyce makes the distinction between these two concepts very effectively

45

when he describes the classical temper as displaying 'security and satisfaction and patience', and the romantic temper as being 'insecure, unsatisfied, impatient'.)

The statement that these three revolutionary movements were dependent upon an emotional appeal may need a fuller explanation. The writers and philosophers who prepared the ground for the French Revolution, men such as Voltaire, Diderot and to a certain extent Rousseau, based their arguments against injustice on Reason. Yet when these ideas were translated into action, the dominant mood was emotional. 'Liberty, Equality, and Fraternity' is a slogan designed to appeal to men's hearts rather than to their rational faculties and, as power passed more and more from the moderates to the extremists and finally to the mob, the shift was complete. A mob never has been and never will be swayed by any other than an emotional appeal, and it took a Napoleon to reintroduce into France even the vestiges of discipline and control.

In terms of religion, Wesley, appalled by what he considered the indolence of the established church and the indifference of the aristocracy to the sufferings of the poor, preached a gospel of salvation through personal conversion. Confining himself largely to the proletariat, his sermons induced in his audiences what the British historian, G. M. Trevelyan, has styled 'convulsions, agonies and raptures'. Whether Wesley intended it or not, the response of congregations with limited theological knowledge had to be emotional. (Wesley himself records that during his addresses, 85 of his listeners 'dropped as dead', a number became temporarily insane and nine succumbed to incurable madness.)

In literature, this same trend is abundantly demonstrated. The two predominant characteristics of the 'romantic' movement are a belief in the holiness of the imagination and a corresponding rejection of reason. The negation of energy and therefore the source of all evil to Blake is 'the Reasoning Power in Man'. His aim is:

> To cast off Rational Demonstration by faith in the Saviour,
> To cast off the rotten rags of Memory by Inspiration,
> To cast off Bacon, Locke and Newton from Albion's covering,
> To take off his filthy garments and clothe him with Imagination,
> To cast aside from Poetry all that is not Inspiration.

This same impatience with restraint and search for an emotional outlet for the imagination can be seen in Wordsworth's definition of poetry as 'the spontaneous overflow of powerful feelings' (though Wordsworth, the most cautious of all the 'romantic' poets, does later add that such 'powerful feelings' are 'recollected in tranquillity'). It can be seen in Keat's remarks in a letter to Benjamin Bailey:

> 'I am certain of nothing but of the holiness of the heart's affections, and the truth of the imagination . . . I have never yet been able to perceive how anything can be known for truth by consecutive reasoning . . . O for a life of sensations rather than of thoughts!'

It can also be seen in the dark, nightmarish symbolism of *The Ancient Mariner* and of *Christabel*, and in the various gothic novels of the period. It may be summed up as a complete rejection of the classical golden mean. 'The road of excess leads to the palace of wisdom', wrote Blake—and as such it has a great deal in common with contemporary literature and thought. Søren Kierkegaard, the acknowledged source of much that has subsequently been formulated under the title of existentialism, echoes the essential mood of 'romanticism' when he states that 'the conclusions of passion are the only reliable ones'.

There is a clearly identifiable link between the movements which culminated in the political, religious and literary revolutions at the end of the 18th century and their present counterparts. The twin forces which characterised these revolutions—anti-authoritarianism and emotionalism—have increased in strength and influence and are the progenitors of the violence and animalism which dominate today's *avant-garde* literature and thought. It may be objected that the political revolution occurred in France, the religious one in England, the literary one in at least three countries; but all are manifestations of the European *Zeitgeist* of the time, which, springing from the same psychic sources, subsequently interacted one upon the other. Blake was kindly disposed towards Methodism and sang the praises of the French Revolution, as did Wordsworth, Coleridge, Shelley and Byron. Generally speaking they all saw Satan, the *non plus ultra* of anti-authoritarianism, as the real 'hero' of *Paradise Lost.* Shelley greatly admired William Godwin's *Political Justice*, which in theory at least advocated the abolition of the monarchy. the class system, property-ownership, marriage, and almost everything else. (Much of the third act of *Prometheus Unbound* is simply Godwin, versified.)

Of major importance is the fact that all three manifestations had a profound impact upon the political, religious and literary life of America, where they reinforced the anti-authoritarianism which, as de Tocqueville pointed out, was already part of the national character. Significantly, it is in America that so much of the modern *avant-garde* movement has evolved or has been avidly and uncritically accepted.[1] Moreover, and

[1] If one examines the names of those who directed literary trends between 1900 and 1960, it would appear that France (Anouilh, Camus, Genet, Gide, Ionesco, Proust, Sartre, Valéry) and America (Albee, Eliot, Faulkner, Ginsberg, Hemingway, Miller,

somewhat ironically, the emergence of America in the past few generations as the political and cultural leader of the West has resulted in what one might term the re-export of such anti-authoritarianism. Consider the example of countless Hollywood films shown around the world in which the well-spoken, cultivated individual is depicted as the villain, whereas the hero displays a mannerless, graceless, ape-like exterior beneath which the audience is induced to believe there lurks a heart of gold. (It is interesting to speculate upon the possible state of contemporary western society had America been founded upon Hobbesian, as opposed to Lockean, concepts of human nature.)

This glorification of the primitive is simply an extension of the 18th-century concept of The Noble Savage, an essential feature of 'romanticism' which Spengler saw as yet another symptom of the decline of a culture :

> 'The soul thinks once again and in Romanticism looks back piteously to its childhood; then finally, weary, reluctant, cold, it loses its desire to be and . . . wishes itself out of the overlong daylight and back in the darkness of proto-mysticism, in the womb of the mother, in the grave'.

There is a startling and alarming similarity between this statement and that of Fiedler in which he sees 'a weariness in the West . . . a weariness with the striving to be men'.

It is tempting, in view of my thesis, to see in the French Revolution and 'romanticism' the catastrophic events which Burke and Spengler do; to view the 18th century as 'the gleaming autumn' of our culture,

---

Pound, Williams) preponderate, with Ireland (Beckett, Joyce, Shaw, Yeats) runner-up. This list, which omits such powerful influences as Brecht, Kafka, and Lawrence, to say nothing of the continuing impact of the psychological theories of Freud and Jung, is obviously incomplete, but it does, nevertheless, reveal something about the sources of 'modernism'.

but this would involve an over-simplification. The 18th century was after all an age of contrasts: civilised, polished, and urbane at the top; brutish, ignorant, down-trodden (and in the English cities, gin-sodden) at the bottom. What distinguished the first half of the century from subsequent ages, however, was the profound belief among the majority of the cultivated that by exercising his powers of reasoning and self-control man could perfect himself. This belief is reflected in the literature of the period, which tends to be moralistic and which manifests an avowed didacticism, qualities hardly likely to appeal to modern readers.

This obvious moralistic and didactic tendency appears to have originated in the Hegelian swing of the pendulum away from the bawdiness and irreligion of the Restoration period. Thus in 1698 the reformer Jeremy Collier, in *A Short View of The Immorality and Profaneness of the English Stage*, declared that

> 'the Business of plays is to recommend virtue and discountenance vice . . . to make Folly and Falsehood contemptible, and to bring every Thing that is Ill under Infamy and Neglect'.

A few years later Joseph Addison stated in the *Spectator:*

> 'For my own part I have endeavoured to make nothing ridiculous, that is not in some measure criminal. I have set up the immoral man as the Object of Derision',

a sentiment echoed by Johnson, who defined a writer's duty as being 'to make the world better'.

The novel, having been until recently essentially a popular literary form, is a useful social reflector, and if we examine the works of the most popular novelist of the period, Samuel Richardson, several significant insights may be obtained. His first novel, *Pamela* (1740), has the revealing sub-title 'Virtue Rewarded' and tells of a servant-girl's successful attempts to escape rape at the hands of her master. So successful is she that he eventually marries her, and in the last two of the four volumes he is depicted as having become under her influence an ideal husband. It is fashionable nowadays to dismiss this book contemptuously as an example of its author's prudential morality. One modern critic has described it as 'procrastinated rape', but this clearly was *not* the message which it had for its contemporary readers. On the title page of the original edition Richardson stated that he was publishing it 'in order to cultivate the Principles of Virtue and Religion in the Minds of the Youth of both Sexes', and Alexander Pope declared that it would do 'more good than many volumes of sermons'.

Although it may strike a modern reader as exhaustingly long and tedious, it enjoyed a fantastic popularity among its contemporaries. Fans, wax-works, plays, and even an opera were constructed on the Pamela theme. Imitations and parodies poured forth and there is no doubt of its extensive influence on the sensibility of the age. The villagers of Slough in Buckinghamshire, for example, who were unable to read, gathered in the village smithy of an evening while the smith read the story to them. When he came to the chapter in which Pamela finally marries her master, the villagers in their enthusiasm swarmed out to the nearby parish church and rang the bells in honour of the wedding. One cannot suppress the suspicion that their modern urban counterparts would be more inclined to such a demonstration were she to be raped.

Richardson's second novel, *Clarissa*, is even longer than *Pamela* and for this reason is now largely neglected, although it is one of the most powerful and effective pieces of writing in our language. The heroine, Clarissa, having run away from home to escape an odious marriage arranged by her parents, is ravished by her 'protector', aptly named Lovelace, and eventually dies, neglected and abandoned. Her seducer is finally killed in a duel by Clarissa's cousin. The didactic nature of the theme is reinforced in the author's preface in which he states that the aim of the book is 'to warn children against preferring a Man of Pleasure to a Man of Probity'.

Having displayed his male characters in a more or less unfavourable role, Richardson obviously felt when he came to write his last novel, *Sir Charles Grandison*, that he needed to depict a hero, a man of elevated sentiments and bearing. In Richardson's words, Grandison exemplifies

> 'a Man acting uniformly well thro' a Variety of trying scenes, because all his Actions are regulated by one steady Principle: A Man of Religion and Virtue; of Liveliness and Spirit; accomplished and agreeable; happy in himself, and a Blessing to others'.

This description reflects its age much as *The Declaration of Independence* reflects American thought in the 1770s. The whole ideal of neo-classicism is summed up in the words 'accomplished and agreeable, happy in himself'; and if the reader should reject all this as mawkish naiveté and assert that Richardson's morality is simply thinly disguised prurience, then possibly he is merely manifesting his own temporal provincialism.

It may be thought that I have devoted too much attention to a largely neglected 18th-century novelist, but Richardson's *Grandison* is an extremely significant literary figure. He reappears in modified form throughout 18th- and 19th-century fiction and is the archetypal hero of the English novel. He survived the onslaught of gothic novels, the self-torturings and introverted agonies of *Young Werthers,* and the posturings of the Byronic heroes, to reappear in the pages of Thackeray,

Trollope and a host of other semi-forgotten Victorians. Today he has no living descendant; his place has been taken by the anti-hero—unaccomplished, disagreeable, unhappy in himself, or by the victim—a helpless creature at the mercy of blind, implacable forces. Jimmy Porter, the protagonist of Osborne's play, is anti-hero and victim rolled into one. It may appear to us unsophisticated and naive that Richardson and his readers should take it for granted that a worthwhile ideal is represented by a man 'accomplished and agreeable; happy in himself, and a Blessing to others', but is it not symptomatic of a far healthier culture than the nervous, introspective and often self-destructive characters typified in contemporary fiction?

The didacticism and moral purport of 18th-century writers were not confined to the novel. From the 'romantic' period on, critics have been justifiably infuriated by some of the tamperings with Shakespeare which began at the end of the 17th century and continued throughout the eighteenth. Foremost among these, certainly the one which has drawn upon itself most contempt and obloquy, is Nahum Tate's version of *King Lear* which was first produced in March, 1681. It is interesting and significant that this version, which had a 'happy ending' (Lear being restored to his Kingdom and Cordelia marrying Edgar), was performed to the exclusion of Shakespeare's *Lear* throughout the entire 18th century and well into the nineteenth. The reason for the rejection of Shakespeare's play was that it failed in Collier's words 'to recommend Virtue, and discountenance Vice'. Johnson is once again very revealing when he censures Shakespeare for sacrificing 'Virtue to Convenience' and adds that he

'is so much more careful to please than to instruct, that he seems to write *without any moral purpose*.' (Italics mine.)

53

Nor was this view confined to literary critics. The philosopher David Hume in his essay *Of Tragedy* (1757), is unequivocal on the subject:

> 'The mere suffering of plaintive virtue, under the triumphant tyranny and oppression of vice, forms a disagreeable spectacle, and is carefully avoided by all masters of the drama.'

We may tend to assume that didacticism is absent from modern literature; the very word has a fusty, old-fashioned flavour repugnant to our sophisticated tastes. But when a philosopher such as Sartre deserts the lecture-hall and writes plays designed to be produced throughout the Western world, it can only be because he wishes to disseminate his views, to put across his ideas to a far wider audience than is possible in the comparatively narrow confines of a university. This is merely another form of didactic literature. There can be little doubt that Sartre's aim, whether he would admit it or not, is to influence people into adopting an existential viewpoint. As T. S. Eliot observed:

> 'The author of a work of imagination is trying to affect us wholly, as human beings, whether he knows it or not; and we are affected by it as human beings, whether we intend to be or not'.

This is true of all writers, regardless of whether their aims be Marxist, moralist, relativist, or even nihilistic, and we forget this as readers or theatre-goers at our peril. The only *real* difference between Richardson's didacticism and that of contemporary writers is that the former's is explicit and therefore less insidious.

Furthermore, our contempt for the moralistic tampering with Shakespeare is yet another instance of our being unable to see the mote in our own eye. Anyone who has attended a recent performance of Shakespeare in London or Stratford-upon-Avon, may on reflection realise that such productions are equally revealing of our age as were those of the 18th century. Today's representations emphasise, predictably, the violent and animalistic aspects in Shakespeare.[1] In other words, all literature, including the productions of plays, appears to reflect the fashions and *mores* of its time, and there are more ways than one of distorting an author's original intentions.

As we have already seen, 'romanticism' rejected most of the ideals of neo-classicism, substituting liberty and emotionalism for restraint and decorum, but if one examines carefully the writings of the major English poets of the period, one can see that the revolt was still incomplete. Nature still provided Wordsworth with the same kind of assurance that it had given Pope. It induced in the former:

> that blessed mood,
> In which the burthen of the mystery,
> In which the heavy and the weary weight
> Of all this unintelligible world,
> Is lightened.

Until eventually the poet states that:

> With an eye made quiet by the power
> Of harmony, and the deep power of joy
> We see into the life of things.

[1] One could cite many examples but the following will be sufficient to illustrate my point. In the 1963 Stratford production of *The Tempest*, which shocked even some hardened drama critics, Caliban was portrayed as almost completely animal.   More blatant was the execution on a gallows *on stage* of the rebels, Worcester and Vernon, in the 1964 production of *Henry IV Part One*, also at Stratford. This directly violates the stage directions— 'Exeunt Worcester and Vernon, guarded'. On the screen the trend is predictably the same. *Playboy* magazine heralded the recent Zeffirelli production of *Romeo & Juliet* as: 'BEAUTIFUL! The entire film is a poem of youth, love and *violence*, . . . a Renaissance *recapitulation* of *West Side Story* played with pure (sic) 1968 passion'. (Italics mine.) Meanwhile, Richard Burton, who was apparently considering producing a new film-version of *Macbeth*, was quoted as saying: 'The script has been written [rewritten?] to give it a little Bonnie and Clyde flavour.'

Although Pope and Wordsworth arrived at their conclusions by different methods, the one by deductive reasoning and the other through a mystical communion with nature, the thoughts expressed are sufficiently similar and indicate what one might loosely describe as an optimistic and reverent cosmic view. This same ambivalence between classicism and 'modernism' can be seen in Shelley. The passage in the third act of *Prometheus Unbound*, in which the Spirit of the Hour recounts the transformation of man from a fawning, self-contemptuous creature into a being 'equal, unclassed, tribeless and nationless . . . the king over himself', anticipates the swing from an external authority to an internal one (self-fulfilment) with remarkable prescience. But contrary to the views of most modern writers man is still regarded as a being essentially capable of nobility, of perfectibility. Indeed, the whole of Shelley's poetry, saturated as it is with classicism (particularly Platonism), is directed towards the ideal of the perfectibility of man. This ideal is of course essentially the same as that of the neo-classicists. Once again, the difference occurs in the method by which such an ideal can be attained. The neo-classicists saw it as an *individual* goal to be reached by reason and self-control; Shelley saw it as a communal one to be accomplished only by the overthrow of despotic forms of tyranny.

The English 'romantics' may have occasionally inverted the yardstick of good and evil (Blake's 'angels' are 'devils' and *vice-versa*), and with perhaps a certain wilful desire to shock they pronounced Satan to be Milton's hero, but the inversion of norms is not the same as their abolition. Satan, with his 'courage, and majesty, and firm and patient opposition to omnipotent force' (Shelley), was a natural choice as their symbol of rebellion, but it is significant that they still regarded him as a hero and not as an anti-hero. In other words, in spite of the powerful reaction to neo-classicism, the 19th-century 'romantics' still inhabited a world more or less intelligible, a world in which men could play heroic roles, partakers of a culture whose norms had not yet been seriously questioned, and this is true of most English and American literature throughout the 19th century.

If a water-shed needs to be defined between the neo-classical age and our own, then it is to Russia that we must turn and, more specifically, to the writings of Fyodor Dostoevsky. It is significant that in Spengler's opinion the next thousand years will belong to Dostoevsky. More cautiously, William McNeill declares in *The Rise Of The West* that Dostoevsky anticipated much that seems characteristic of the 20th century. For at a time when few western Europeans doubted the intrinsic superiority of their cultural inheritance, Dostoevsky's generation of Russian intellectuals found it impossible easily and automatically to accept any single cultural universe. Specifically, I wish to draw attention to certain passages from his *Notes from Underground*. This book published just over a century ago is the true precursor of what one might call the modern literary movement. In it, for example, the term 'anti-hero' is first used.

In *Prometheus Unbound*, Prometheus confronted by the foul furies asks wonderingly : 'Can aught exult in its deformity?' to which Dostoevsky's Underground Man answers with a soul-searing affirmative : 'I am a sick man . . . I am a spiteful man. I am an unpleasant man', and adds that his only enjoyment reposes 'in the hyper-consciousness' of his 'own degradation'. The more conscious he is 'of goodness and of all that "sublime and beautiful" ', the more deeply and gloatingly he sinks 'into the mire'. Like Jimmy Porter and his confrères, he

appears to revel in his own lack of goodness and dignity
while denying that anyone is better than he is:

> 'I am a blackguard, because I am the nastiest, stupidest,
> pettiest, absurdest and most envious of all worms on earth,
> none of whom is a bit better than I am.'

Here, then, is Underground Man exulting in his soul-
sickness and animalism, comparing himself and all
mankind to worms and taking apparent pride in the fact
that he is baring his soul in public, stripping himself to a
state of spiritual nudity.[1] In this respect, Dostoevsky's
character is the prototype of the contemporary proletarian anti-hero, and the protagonists of Dostoevsky and
Osborne both reveal the same desire to degrade themselves, to strip themselves of all pretensions and to
wallow in their own despair and self-pity. 'The dignity
of thinking beings', Johnson's phrase, would be utterly
meaningless to them; the Underground Man and Porter
would alike greet it with contemptuous laughter. But
the laughter is hollow, for they are aware of a sense of
loss—the loss of an ideal.

---

[1] He also exemplifies the sado-masochistic mentality to which I
have previously referred: '. . . in despair occur the most intense
enjoyments, especially when one is very acutely conscious of
one's hopeless position'. Elsewhere he asserts that 'whether it's
good or bad, it is sometimes very pleasant to smash things'.

4 The Reasons Why

'Now there are times when a whole generation is caught ...
between two ages, between two modes of life and thus loses
the feeling for itself, for the self-evident, for all morals, for
being safe and innocent.'

Hermann Hesse : *Steppenwolf* (1929)

It is remarkable how the above quotation echoes the
sentiments expressed by Matthew Arnold in 'Stanzas
From The Grande Chartreuse', composed some 74 years
previously. Arnold, mourning the fact that 'rigorous
teachers seized his youth and purged its faith, and
trimmed its fire', describes his generation of intellectuals
as :

> Wandering between two worlds, one dead,
> The other powerless to be born.

and expresses the hope that :

> Years hence, perhaps, may dawn an age,
> More fortunate, alas ! than we,
> Which without hardness will be sage.
> And gay without frivolity.
> Sons of the world, oh, speed those years ;
> But, while we wait, allow our tears !

The loss to which Arnold is referring arose from his
growing inability to believe in an ordering, controlling,
cosmic intelligence, or in other words, a God. This
failure of belief (for which Arnold attempted to substitute culture, believing that only in this way could

anarchy be avoided), was confined in his day to a small if growing minority; today it has become as fixed and dominant in Western thought as were belief and faith in previous ages. This statement may be challenged by impressive statistics regarding church-attendance, but church-going and genuine faith in a personal and supernatural God bear little relationship to one another.

A few years ago I discussed John Robinson's *Honest To God* with a group of students at a church-related college. They were intelligent, articulate, if somewhat earnest, young people, but when we came to the passage in which Robinson alludes to Julian Huxley's sense of spiritual relief on rejecting the idea of God 'as a supernatural being', I found that the students did not need to reject any such belief. They had never had it. What had taken Robinson and others of his generation years of heart-searching and mental anguish to achieve, they had effortlessly assumed and had been waiting for him, or someone else, to articulate their position. All of them were regular church-goers and no doubt participated in the singing of such hymns as Addison's 'The spacious firmament on high' (with its concluding line, 'The hand that made us is divine'), without realising the essential incongruity of their attitude.

Theological controversy is not the chief purpose of the present study, but two important points deserve attention. Firstly, Arnold's sense of loss appears to have become a gain for Huxley. Secondly, no real understanding of modern literature or society is possible without recognising that for the vast majority of modern writers, artists, critics and other moulders of public tastes and beliefs, God, in the old sense of the word, is not dead but never existed. Furthermore, anyone who professes such a belief in a supernatural force is, in their opinion, either an escapist (that is to say, a moral coward), or else lacks the intellectual apparatus to give his opinion weight.

In consequence, a form of intellectual totalitarianism has been established, within which charmed circle everything is condoned and no limits are imposed upon its members' actions or beliefs. Any attempt to impose such restrictions would be greeted with cries of 'censorship' or 'fascism'; yet curiously enough they, themselves, constitute a new *Herrenvolk* or master race. One has only to substitute the terms 'Western culture' or 'the past', for 'non-Aryan' in Nazi writings, and the comparison will not seem so extravagant. Lest some readers may feel that I exaggerate the hostility of the moderns to traditional culture and values, the following passage from *The Dehumanisation of Art* (1925) by Ortega y Gasset may lend support for my statement:

'For about twenty years now the most alert young people of two successive generations—in Berlin, Paris, London, New York, Rome, Madrid—have found themselves faced with the undeniable fact that they have no use for traditional art; moreover, that they detest it'.

He goes on to observe that hatred of art is unlikely to be an isolated phenomenon:

'it goes hand in hand with hatred of science, hatred of State, hatred, in sum, of civilisation as a whole'.

One may recall that this total rejection of tradition and of traditional morality and religion signified, in Spengler's opinion, the death-throes of a culture and of a civilisation.

Only with an understanding of the almost total secularisation of Western society during the past century do such modern philosophical, religious, and literary phenomena as Existentialism,[1] Situational

---

[1] I am not referring here to such 'religious existentialists' as Gabriel Marcel, Martin Buber, Karl Jaspers and Paul Tillich, but rather to that type of existentialism typified by Jean-Paul Sartre. The latter has enjoyed, for fairly obvious reasons, a much greater

Ethics, and the Theatre of the Absurd become intelligible. They are all in differing ways manifestations of a failure to believe in a Supreme Being and, therefore, in a regulated, ordered universe. The abandonment of the old moral sanctions in a search for self-fulfilment is yet another result of this loss of faith. As I. A. Richards has observed:

> 'When a created, simple and eternal soul was the pivotal point, Good was conformity with the will of the creator, Evil was rebellion. When the associationist psychologists substituted a swarm of sensations and images for the soul, Good becomes pleasure and Evil becomes pain'.

He adds that what differentiates good from evil is that one represents 'fullness' and the other 'narrowness'.

Of additional importance is the fact that with the loss of faith, more and more writers and artists are repudiating, either overtly or tacitly, the belief in man's spirituality and are concentrating exclusively upon his animalistic qualities.

Tennyson was one of the last of the major writers to exhibit an affirmative belief in man's destiny; in the conclusion of *In Memoriam* he bids man

> . . . Arise and fly
> The reeling Faun, the sensual feast;
> Move upward, working out the beast,
> And let the ape and tiger die.

Nowadays such hope seems absent. Contemporary writers dwell upon 'the sensual feast' and appear ignorant, for the most part, of even the possibility of an alternative.

I have said that such modern phenomena as Existen-

---

popularity in literary circles than have the former. Moreover, since Camus' opinions differ markedly from those of Sartre (he once declared that he did not have 'much liking for the too famous existential philosophy'), his whole philosophy will be treated in a subsequent chapter (Chapter 7).

tialism, Situational Ethics, and the Theatre of the Absurd are only intelligible in the context of this loss of faith in an external and eternal God. In other words they subsist on the belief that this life is all we have. In order to elaborate upon this statement, I propose to examine each of these phenomena, separately, as a manifestation of our 'Godless' society.

The existentialist (and again I am not referring here to religious existentialism') regards the earth and the entire universe as random, accidental and therefore meaningless phenomena, devoid of any significance or morality. Man does, however, retain a measure of choice; when confronted by this cosmic inanity he can decide either to 'lead an enthusiastic and honourable existence' (the phrase is William Barrett's), or he can lapse into despair. The atheistic basis for such philosophy is too obvious to need elaboration, but certain questions remain unanswered. First of all, if surrounded by such overwhelming chaos on all sides, why bother to make a choice, particularly since in the final analysis all such decisions are meaningless and therefore obviously void? Sartre, himself, appears to have reached this spiritual nadir when he declares in *St. Genet* that 'we are in any event impossible nullities'. Tennyson has a more realistic reaction to the problem, when, after contemplating the possibility of such a meaningless, soulless universe, he declares:

> . . . 'Twere hardly worth my while to choose
> Of things all mortal, or to use
> A little patience ere I die;
>
> 'Twere best at once to sink to peace,
> Like birds the charming serpent draws,
> To drop head-foremost in the jaws
> Of vacant darkness and to cease.
>   (*In Memoriam*)

The fact that Sartre and his followers do not pursue Tennyson's course suggests that, either they have not faced up to the full implications of their beliefs (or more properly, disbeliefs), or alternatively they have discovered some palliative, such as Communism, in the furtherance of which they can escape from the knowledge of the futility of absolutely everything, including, of course, the futility of whichever fashionable escapist activity is currently engrossing their attention. Such a philosophy may sustain itself *for a time*, living on its own dynamism, but eventually the persistent, questioning 'why?' will arise, and with no adequate answer the edifice must crumble. Secular activists resemble players in a football game in which there are no rules, no referee, no time-limit and no spectators; for a time a certain physical exuberance will keep the participants occupied, but as their energy becomes sapped, so the purposelessness of the whole game will permeate their consciousness and one by one they will retire, leaving only the totally unintelligent and insensitive to continue the endless farce. As Teilhard de Chardin has written in *The Phenomenon of Man*:

> 'Even on stacks of material energy, even under the spur of immediate fear or desire, *without the taste for life*, mankind would soon stop inventing and constructing for a work it knew to be doomed in advance ... If progress is a myth, that is to say, if faced by the work involved we can say: "What's the good of it all?" our efforts will flag'.

Secondly, when faced with a cosmic inanity which reduces man to an 'impossible nullity', why attempt to reduce such chaos to a system? Why not lie back and scream or indulge in any other maniacal act which has presumably as much or as little significance as philosophical speculation or any other rational activity? Why write plays and short stories? Why not abandon oneself to suicide or an avowed, conscious hedonism? To attempt anything else while holding such views is simply compounding absurdity. We cannot have it both ways. Either there is a controlling force, lending meaning and significance to the universe and to individual and collective human life or else, to quote Tennyson again, the 'earth is darkness at the core, and dust and ashes all that is'.

In this light, Huxley's sense of spiritual relief which comes from rejecting the idea 'of God as a supernatural being' appears to be totally unintelligible; whereas Arnold's anguish would seem to stem from a far more honest confrontation with the awesome and over-whelming implications of such a view. It appears that, in spite of their avowed attitude, most existentialists do indicate a preference for certain modes of conduct as opposed to others; do recognise certain actions as being inherently 'good' while others are 'bad', and so on. If pressed for an explanation, they fall back upon 'instinct' or quote Kierkegaard's remark that 'the conclusions of passion are the only reliable ones'. But whence the instinct? And why in a random, chaotic universe should there be any 'conclusions' arising from 'passion' and why should they be 'reliable'? One cannot but feel that, if further pressed, they would be forced to fall back on a position not dissimilar to that which Pope expresses in the *Essay on Man* :

> This light and darkness in our chaos joined,
> What shall divide? The God within the mind.

Next, let us consider Situational Ethics as another manifestation of the contemporary failure to accept a supernatural deity or divine order. Julian Huxley concedes that

'every society, in every age, needs some system of beliefs, including a basic attitude to life, an organised set of ideas round which emotion and purpose may gather, and a conception of human destiny. It needs a philosophy and a faith to achieve a guide to orderly living—in other words a morality'.

Situational Ethics is an attempt to provide a basis for personal morality which may vary according to the situation in which the individual finds himself at a given moment, as opposed to the old legalistic code which held to certain, inexorable, unchanging laws of conduct. Thus situational ethicists are relativistic : in the words of their most recent spokesman, Joseph Fletcher, they deny 'that there are . . . any unwritten immutable laws of heaven', agreeing with Rudolf Bultmann 'that all such notions are idolatrous and a demonic pretension'. As Fletcher points out in *Situation Ethics*, 'Judaism, Catholicism and Protestantism, all major Western religious traditions have been legalistic'. In other words, Situational Ethics, as a system, is yet another attack on traditional morality.

Fletcher himself obviously recognises the danger of lapsing into antinomianism or amorality :

'To be relative of course means to be relative to something. To be absolutely relative . . . is to be inchoate, random, unpredictable, unjudgeable, meaningless, amoral . . . There must be an absolute or norm of some kind if there is to be any true relativity'.

Let us examine now a typical example, cited by Fletcher, of Situational Ethics applied to a concrete case. While trekking west, along the Boone trail in Kentucky in the 18th century, two families are separated from the wagon-train. A woman has an ailing child who is endangering her and her other three children by its constant cries. Nevertheless, she clings to the child whose noise eventually betrays their presence to some Indians who capture and kill them. Another woman, recognising that her crying baby is endangering the trail party, kills it with her bare hands and they are able to reach their destination in safety. Which woman, Fletcher asks, made the correct decision ? I suspect that

the vast majority of readers would agree with Fletcher
that the second woman showed courage and sagacity.
True, she broke one of the Ten Commandments; but
relative to her situation, who can doubt that she acted
in an understandable manner? Few would realise that
in taking this position they are, in fact, denying the
existence of anything beyond this life; that they are
emphasising the 'here and now' and repudiating the
possibility of a hereafter; that they are placing the
fallible, finite, human mind in the position of an infinite,
eternal one.

The exponents of such a system do not appear to see
that if you take away the idealistic foundation on which
religion has been built, that is to say, an external,
personal, supernatural, spiritual being, the whole edifice
collapses. Where is the source of the 'absolute or norm'
without which all is 'inchoate, random, unpredictable,
unjudgeable, meaningless'? The problem for them is
essentially the same as it is for the existentialists. How
does one create any sense out of chaos? Why bother
to try? Fletcher takes issue, predictably, with Cicero's
statement in *De Legibus* to the effect that

> 'only a madman could maintain that the distinction between
> the honourable and dishonourable, between virtue and vice,
> is a matter of opinion, not of nature'.

But this, says Fletcher, is exactly what Situation Ethics
maintains. In other words, every man can establish his
own private system of morality; Sartre can canonise
Genet, a self-confessed pervert and thief; Mailer can
encourage people to 'develop the psychopath' in themselves; non-art can be made into art and so forth.

A belief in God (as ultimate reference), results in an
assumption that there exist ultimate moral, aesthetic
and legal standards. Conversely, a lack of such belief
eventually creates a society in which every individual

becomes his own moralist, aesthete and law-maker. The outcome of such supra-individualism is social and artistic anarchy, a state into which Western society and possibly mankind as a whole appears to be rushing.[1]

One other point is of prime significance. Both Sartre and Fletcher emphasise *violence* in the situations they utilise to expound their beliefs. In Sartre's *The Wall*, three men have been condemned to death before a firing-squad during the Spanish Civil War and the story recounts in clinical detail their actions and emotions throughout the night prior to their execution. In *No Exit*, Garcin has died at the hands of a firing-squad, Estelle has murdered her baby, Inez died when her lesbian friend turned on the gas in their room. Fletcher's example of the two women cut off from the wagon-train is typical of many which he uses. Both writers would no doubt maintain that violence dramatises the situation and that, living in a violent world, it would be intellectually and socially dishonest to depict life in any other way.

If, however, in the novels which he reads, in the plays and films which he sees, and in the philosophical and ethical treatises which are presented for his edification, Western man is *continually* subjected to a vision of himself as a being violent, animalistic, alienated, mannerless and uncivilised, then is he not being encouraged to identify himself with such an image and mould his own outlook and behaviour to conform with

[1] An article, 'Ezra Pound And The Great Style', by Hayden Carruth (*Saturday Review*, 9 April 1966), made this point forcefully. 'What meaning', he asks, 'has Homer or Ezra Pound in an age of inverting values? . . . How shall our children live in a world from which the spirit, then history and finally nature have fled, leaving only the mindless mechanics of process and chance? Will any place exist for a humane art in a society from which the last trace of reverence—any reverence—has been rubbed out?'

such image? Is there not a real danger that, like Prometheus, we will 'grow like what [we] contemplate and laugh and stare in loathsome sympathy?' Man is, largely, what he conceives himself to be and the facts are incontrovertible. While the exponents of Situational Ethics stress the doctrine of every man his own moralist, crimes, particularly crimes involving violence, increase and a wave of savagery threatens to engulf our civilisation. After examining the real implications of Existentialism and Situational Ethics, one can perhaps sympathise with T. S. Eliot's remarks in 'Thoughts After Lambeth':

> 'The world is trying the experiment of attempting to form a civilised but non-Christian mentality. The experiment will fail, but we must be very patient in awaiting its collapse; meanwhile redeeming the time; so that the Faith may be preserved alive through the dark ages before us; to renew and rebuild civilisation, and save the World from suicide'.

Ortega y Gasset draws attention to an essential flaw in relativism, when he observes in *The Modern Theme*, that

> 'if truth does not exist, relativism cannot take itself seriously ... belief in truth is a deeply-rooted foundation of human life; if we remove it, life is converted into an illusion and an absurdity'.

It is from an inability to conceive of life as anything but an illusion and an absurdity that the Theatre of the Absurd originates. Its advocates argue, much as the existentialists do, that since there is no transcendent being, and therefore no universal plan, man is a random creature whose futile attempts to impose order on the surrounding chaos are merely absurd. He is seen as a victim at the mercy of an indifferent (if not hostile) cosmos.

Although associated with such modern playwrights as Ionesco, Hildesheimer and Dürrenmatt, the Theatre of the Absurd had its genesis in Paris at the end of the last century, when Alfred Jarry's play, *Ubu Roi*, was produced at the Théâtre Nouveau in 1896. This drama, grotesque by any standards of its time, bears a certain superficial resemblance in plot to *Macbeth*, but beyond that the comparison between Jarry and Shakespeare ends. Père Ubu, the embodiment of stupidity, brutality, and ferocity, murders King Wenceslas of Poland, and having gained the throne with the assistance of his wife, terrorises the country, until he is finally defeated in battle by the Czar of Russia, who has allied himself with Bougrelas, the son and sole survivor of Wenceslas's family. The play ends with Père Ubu and his wife on a ship headed for France.[1]

Violence and animalism are the dominating themes, as the following extracts from the opening scene illustrate; they will also provide an idea of the general quality of the dialogue.

Père Ubu. Shittr![2]

Mère Ubu. Oh! That's a nice way to talk. Père Ubu, ye are a bloody great oaf.

Père Ubu. Why don't I bash your brains in, Mère Ubu.

Mère Ubu. It's not me you ought to do in, Père Ubu, it's someone else.

Père Ubu. By my green candle, I don't understand.

Mère Ubu. Well, Père Ubu, are ye content with your lot?

Père Ubu. By my green candle, shittr, Madame, certainly I am content . . .

Mère Ubu. Who's stopping you from slaughtering the whole family and putting yourself in their place?

Père Ubu. Oh! Mère Ubu, you insult me, and you'll find yourself in the stewpan in a minute.

Mère Ubu. Huh! You poor fish, if I found myself in the stewpan, who'd mend the seat of your breeches?

Père Ubu. Well, what of it? Isn't my arse the same as anyone else's?

---

[1] *Ubu Roi* is really the first of a trilogy, the others being *Ubu cocu* (1897) and *Ubu enchainé* (published in 1900).

[2] In the original, 'merdre'.

Later in the scene Mère Ubu soliloquises as follows:

> 'Fart, shittr, it's hard to get him moving, but fart, shittr, I
> reckon I've shaken him all the same. Thanks to God and
> myself, in a week, maybe, I'll be Queen of Poland.'

Jarry's intention was obviously to shock his audience
and in this he was eminently successful; it is, however,
open to doubt if the play has any other merit. Ubu's
'disembraining' machine, his mass impalings of his
enemies and the casual cruelty that permeates the play
were obviously a deliberate theatrical attempt at protest,
but one is permitted to ask at what particular social,
religious or political abuse the protest is directed?
George Wellwarth, in *The Theatre of Protest and
Paradox*, equates Ubu with the 'cosmic malignant force
that pervades the *avant-garde* drama' and adds that
when Jarry wrote the play 'he was rebelling not only
against the outmoded conventions of the current drama
. . . but against absolutely everything' including 'the
world and the cosmos'.

The futility of this is too obvious to need comment,
yet it is surely significant that interest in Jarry (and also
in De Sade with whom Jarry shares certain characteristics) has grown in recent years and that in 1948 a
'College of "Pataphysics" ' was founded in his honour.
He, himself, carried his protest to its logical (or illogical)
end by deliberately drinking himself to death at the age
of thirty-four, having gravitated from alcohol to ether.
Gabriel Brunet has said that Jarry's teaching can be
summarised as follows:

> 'Every man is capable of showing his contempt for the cruelty
> and stupidity of the universe by making his own life a poem of
> *incoherence and absurdity.*'[1] (Italics mine.)

---

[1] It is interesting to note that Camus, in the fourth of his *Lettres à
un ami allemand* (1944), attributes the rise of Nazism to the
moral chaos created by an *awareness of the absurdity* of life.

Commenting on *Ubu Roi*, Wellwarth sees it as the genesis of the *avant-garde* drama and rightly observes that in such drama the power to shock is its chief source of strength; it is also its greatest weakness, because it is self-consuming. What shocks an audience today will be acceptable tomorrow and thus the contemporary dramatist is constantly impelled to seek further excesses to gratify a warped taste which he has himself implanted in the public mind.

Shall tomorrow's playwright boldly depict males embracing on the stage? It has already been done in Osborne's *A Patriot for Me*. Shall he have a man publicly castrate himself? Genet's *The Balcony* has anticipated him. Shall he display a woman urinating on the stage? Picasso's *Le Désir Attrapé par la Queue* has forestalled him. Shall he stage his play in a lunatic asylum, a public urinal, a brothel? All such locales have already been exploited. The possible avenues for original obscenity and scatology are one by one being cut off, and one wonders how the jaded theatrical palates of the future will be titillated. The contemporary playwright or producer might well take as his motto, 'Après moi, la sécheresse', and congratulate himself that he is writing before a morbid public appetite demands scenes of such repellent realism that actors and actresses will have to be killed on the stage in order to satisfy it.

The Theatre of Cruelty is simply an extension of this trend and is as self-consuming as the Theatre of the Absurd. Both depend upon shock, upon the ability to pander to the baser instincts in man; and this is true no matter how philosophic the theories of its exponents may superficially appear to be. Wellwarth, indeed, appears to concede this when he defines the chief philosophical standpoint of contemporary *avant-garde* drama as 'death-oriented hopelessness'; but it is difficult to accept the styling of such an attitude 'philosophic', and, as George Santayana observed, 'spiritual anguish . . . cannot be banished by spiritual anarchy'.

One other point needs to be mentioned. An *avant-garde* is, by definition, an advanced group which goes ahead of the main body under the assumption that the majority will follow later. In this respect Dryden in his day was *avant-garde*, so were Wordsworth and Coleridge; but what they rejected were the literary traditions of the previous ages. Today's *avant-garde* rejects the whole basis of society and, indeed, rejects the very society on which it preys. To this extent, it could more properly be styled a cultural guerilla group, owing allegiance to no one save its own members, contemptuous not only of the main body but also of civilisation and civilised behaviour.

Arnold Toynbee in his *Study of History* states that the breakdowns of civilisations can be summed up in three defects:

> 'a failure of creative power in the minority, an answering withdrawal of mimesis [i.e. imitation] on the part of the majority, and a consequent loss of social unity in the society as a whole'.

If we are *not* affected by contemporary literature, drama and so forth, then there is a 'withdrawal of mimesis', and our civilisation is in danger of breaking down. On the other hand, if we are affected by them, it is surely worth our while to examine carefully the images on which we are moulding our behaviour.

Trilling asserts that

> 'whenever in modern literature we find violence . . . and an insistence upon the sordid and disgusting and an insult offered to the prevailing morality or habit of life, we may assume that we are in the presence of the intention to destroy specious good'.

But why must one assume this ? Is iconoclasm always a virtue, and, even assuming it to be, are authors and playwrights immune to the danger that in the process they may become contaminated by their own material and descend to obscenity for obscenity's sake ?

One cannot overlook the possible relevance of Johnson's dictum that 'no man but a blockhead ever wrote except for money', and certainly, 'whenever in modern literature we find violence . . . and an insistence upon the sordid and disgusting', we are also in the presence of a potential best-seller or box-office success.[1] The amount of such literature is far greater in capitalist countries, where it is an extremely profitable business, and the continuing growth of a large section of the public which has acquired literacy without taste would appear to ensure even bigger profits in the future. It is also worth noting the term 'specious good' in Trilling's statement. Whilst the majority of these writers would deny the validity of any moral absolutes, they are seemingly able to distinguish between true and specious good and are attempting to impose such minority opinions upon the majority. In an open society we may concede that this is their right, but one remains at liberty to doubt whether the ordinary novel-reader or theatre-goer is sufficiently sophisticated to draw such profound implications or whether he sees anything

---

[1] In an article, 'European Literary Review' (*Saturday Review*, 6 January, 1968), Alan Sillitoe, author of *Saturday Night and Sunday Morning, The Loneliness of the Long Distance Runner*, etc., and formerly one of Britain's angriest young men, was described as breakfasting at an exclusive Tangier hotel, 'sipping coffee and cognac'. He was reported to be feeling guilty about his success: 'What would the comrades of Nottingham do if they could see me having my cigar lit and my shoes shined by the Moroccan proletariat ?' Presumably, if the 'comrades' had read *Animal Farm* they would not be too surprised.

other than men and women behaving like animals—trousered or indeed untrousered apes.

In *The Abolition of Man*, C. S. Lewis takes issue with the modern concept of relativism in literature, aesthetics, and morality. He maintains that certain objects *are* sublime in their own right quite apart from man's reactions to them:

'Until quite modern times all teachers and even all men believed the universe to be such that certain emotional reactions on our part could be either congruous or incongruous to it, believed, in fact, that objects did not merely receive, but could *merit* our approval or disapproval, our reverence, or our contempt'.

Similarly, certain ways of life were held to be good, while others were innately wrong or bad. This code Lewis refers to as the *Tao*, which he defines as:

'the doctrine of objective value, the belief that certain attitudes are really true and others really false to the kind of thing the universe is and the kind of things we are'.[1]

Basically, his idea is derived from Aristotle who, in the *Nichomachean Ethics*, having pointed out that a stone can never be trained to resist falling to earth even if one throws it up ten thousand times, states that man is similarly adapted by his nature to receive the virtues

[1] Support for this view is apparent in some anthropological studies. The late Clyde Kluckhohn, formerly of Harvard University, states:

'Contrary to the statements of Ruth Benedict and other exponents of extreme cultural relativity, standards and values are not completely relative to the cultures from which they derive. Some values are as much givens in human life as the fact that bodies of certain densities fall under specified conditions. These are founded, in part, upon the fundamental biological similarities of all human beings. They arise also out of the circumstance that human existence is invariably a social existence. No society has ever approved suffering as a good thing in itself . . . No culture fails to put a negative valuation upon killing, indiscriminate lying, and stealing within the in-group . . . Nor need we dispute the universality of the conception that rape or any achievement of sexuality by violent means is disapproved'. *(continued on page 54)*

which 'are made perfect by habit'. This *Tao* embraces the platonic, Christian, and Oriental philosophies and it is only comparatively recently that man has questioned its essential rightness as a guide to civilised behaviour.

This does *not*, of course, mean that there were not social critics in previous ages. Indeed, many of those whose teachings have helped to formulate the *Tao* made extreme strictures upon their contemporary societies— Socrates and Christ, for example. But what differentiates these from the majority of moderns is that, even when most critical, they never questioned that there was such a thing as good, just as there was evil, that there was a right way and a wrong way for a man to lead his life. Voltaire, that arch-iconoclast of the 18th century realised the necessity of the *Tao* when he wrote: 'If God did not exist, it would be necessary to invent him'.

Most contemporary writers have gone to the ultimate extreme and have questioned the whole fabric of the *Tao* as a guide to life, and have rejected it. This has resulted in dark pessimism and finally nihilism—'the death-oriented hoplessness' to which Wellwarth refers. Both these attitudes have, of course, been expressed

---

Kluckhohn also points out that conceptions of 'the mentally normal' have common elements. 'The "normal" individual must have a certain measure of control over his impulse life. The person who threatens the lives of his neighbours without socially approved justification is always and everywhere treated either as insane or as a criminal.' Of great importance to the concept of the *Tao* is the following: 'The very fact that all cultures have had their categorical imperatives that went beyond mere survival and immediate pleasure is one of vast significance . . . The word *universal* is preferable to *absolute* because whether or not a value is universal can be determined empirically. Some values may indeed be absolute because of the unchanging nature of man or the inevitable conditions of human life.' ('Values and Value-Orientations in the Theory of Action', *Toward A General Theory of Action*, ed. Talcott Parsons and Edward A. Shils.)

in the past. The speaker in *Ecclesiastes* declared that he had 'seen all the works that are done under the sun' and 'behold, all is vanity and vexation of the spirit'. Macbeth, hearing of his wife's suicide and conscious of the approach of MacDuff's avenging armies, gave vent to one of the most anguished and nihilistic outbursts in literature. Life for him at that moment was merely 'a tale told by an idiot, full of sound and fury, signifying nothing'. No modern has managed to express the utter loneliness and alienation of man better than Shakespeare. But *Ecclesiastes* is not the *whole* of the Bible, nor is all of Shakespeare nihilistic. There is a balance of light and dark, of hope and despair, of sublimity and degradation in these works which is absent from modern literature : Yeats, lamenting the loss of what he called 'Unity of Culture', asked despairingly : 'Why are these strange souls born everywhere today ? with hearts that Christianity, as shaped by history, cannot satisfy', and added : 'Why should we believe that religion can never bring round its antithesis ?' This question, today, seems superfluous, with conditions appearing to conspire to bring about the vision which Yeats, himself, expressed in 1919, in 'The Second Coming' :

> Things fall apart, the centre cannot hold :
> Mere anarchy is loosed upon the world,
> The blood-dimmed tide is loosed, and everywhere
> The ceremony of innocence is drowned.

5 The 'Raskolnikovian' Mind

'Despair, fed by the prejudices of hallucination, imperturbably leads literature to the mass abrogation of laws both social and divine, and to theoretical and practical wickedness.'

Lautréamont: *Poésies*

I have stated that theological considerations are secondary in this book, believing that an argument between an atheist and a believer resembles a dispute between two pygmies as to what lies on the other side of a 60-foot wall. The existence of God can neither be proved nor disproved and there always remains what Browning calls 'The grand Perhaps'. In explaining the atheism which I have suggested was implicit in such modern phenomena as Existentialism, Situational Ethics, and The Theatre of the Absurd, most observers would probably cite the growth of science and 'rationalism' as the main factors. I. A. Richards, for example, describes the central dominant change between our age and previous ones as the '*Naturalisation* of *Nature*, the transference from the Magical View of the world to the scientific', and it would indeed be unwise to ignore the cumulative effect of Lyell, Darwin, Freud, Nietzsche, Pavlov, Marx, Russell *et al.* upon modern consciousness.

On the other hand, as John Robinson has pointed out, there is nothing to stop us locating God beyond

> 'the limit set to "space" by the speed of light . . . And there he would be quite invulnerable and in a "gap" science could never fill'.

Robinson is speaking ironically, but he does suggest that the failure to believe in a transcendent, immanent Being cannot be explained solely in terms of advances in scientific knowledge. Science and 'rationalism' have still to explain what the deists called 'The great First Cause'—that *mysterium tremendum et fascinosum*— and it would seem that there are other less obvious reasons for such lack of belief, and once again Dostoevsky supplies a possible clue as to their source.

I am not here concerned with Dostoevsky's motives in writing *Crime and Punishment*. Some would maintain that, although superficially it is a polemic against the radical generation of nihilistic Russian intellectuals, its author, consciously or subconsciously, identifies himself with Raskolnikov in his rebellion. 'Raskol' means 'dissent', and this above all is what the protagonist represents. He feels alienated from his family, from his studies, from his former friends, and from society as a whole. One might say that not only was he born to be a dissenter, but also had dissent thrust upon him by his environment. It is no coincidence that the crime takes place in St Petersburg, the symbol of an abstract, planned city,[1] violating the old Russian traditions, and it is among the foetid slums of this city that Raskolnikov commits his double murder, the motive for which he is subsequently unable to explain.

Following the murders he does attempt to rationalise his motives, but each time he reaches an explanation he immediately rejects it and continues to search for

[1] The speaker in *Notes From Underground* refers to St Petersburg as 'the most abstract and intentional city in the world'.

ano⁺her. Did he murder for financial gain ? from hunger ? from a desire to prove himself a superman, above the law and conventional morality ? One can only conclude that he killed from an obsessive and compulsive need to destroy, even though in the process he also destroyed himself : 'Did I murder the old woman ?' he asks, and in a moment of self-realisation answers his own question : 'I murdered myself not her.' The parallel between Raskolnikov and Alfred Jarry is interesting. The latter, too, destroyed himself in a similar compulsive manner, in a vain protest against the cosmos. Raskolnikov is seen by the magistrate as 'a modern case' and in his peculiar blend of sadism and masochism, in his emotional extremism, he is still an easily recognisable, contemporary literary and social phenomenon.

The American novelist and critic, Susan Sontag, in an article on the contemporary novel makes the following observation :

> 'One of the primary features of literature (as of much activity in all the other arts) in our time is a chronic attachment to materials belonging to the realm of "extreme situations": madness, crime, taboo sexual longings, drug addiction, emotional degradation, violent death'.

With the exceptions of the taboo sexual longings and drug addiction, these are the ingredients of *Crime and Punishment*, and Raskolnikov appears to be as archetypal a figure as the speaker in *Notes From Underground*. One passage from the former novel deserves particular attention ; it is spoken by Pyotr Petrovich Luzhin, the odious, calculating fiancé of Raskolnikov's sister Dounia :

> 'New valuable ideas, new valuable works are circulating in the place of our old dreamy and romantic authors. Literature is taking a maturer form, many injurious prejudices have been rooted up and turned into ridicule . . . In a word, we have cut ourselves off irrevocably from the past, and that, to my thinking, is a great thing. . . .'

Dostoevsky's intention here is obviously satiric; he is attacking the new breed of Russian intellectuals, the theorists who were espousing the secular trend, rationalistic, utilitarian, crudely materialistic, that asserted itself in mid-century Russia.

The ideas Pyotr Petrovich expressed in this passage originated among the dissident intellectual class, and the irony is that he, the symbol of the calculating bourgeois, should be parroting them without understanding their real significance. 'He's learnt it by heart to show off!' is Raskolnikov's immediate reaction to Petrovich's words. Precisely the same phenomenon is observable in contemporary intellectual and bourgeois circles. The latter class, under the influence of the former, is being made to feel ashamed not only of its vices but also of its virtues, and, contrary to all human experience and common sense, is beginning to doubt if there exists any real difference between the two. I have referred to the danger to youth inherent in some of the abstract theories which, available to all but understood by few, are flooding the book shops. Contemporary ideas need to be weighed not against others of the same period but against those of the past, and it is here that the average, modern student is defenceless. His interests and leisure reading are confined to an alarming extent to contemporary writers and thinkers who, despite their apparent individualism, are all really working in the same direction. It is ironic that the current demand at universities is for more relevance (that is to say, contemporaneity) in the curriculum. If acceded to, this will result in a still larger degree of temporal provincialism and an even more profound ignorance of the history of ideas than now prevails.

To return to Raskolnikov, it would seem that his real motive was to destroy a segment of that society from which he felt alienated and rejected, even if in the process he destroyed the better part of himself. As I have suggested, this blend of sado-masochism is a dominant one in contemporary intellectualism as the growing revival in popularity of De Sade and Jarry illustrates. And is it not possible that our contemporary inability to believe in a God and in an ordered, controlled universe is yet another manifestation of the cult of unpleasure? After all, in the absence of proof to the contrary, would it not be preferable to believe? As Browning's Bishop Blougram puts it to the sceptical Gigadibs, 'it's best believing, if we may; You can't but own that!' There is a *will* to disbelieve today, just as in former ages the converse was true, and we would appear to be deliberately bringing upon ourselves that 'moral chaos' which a withdrawal from God implies.[1] One cannot but recall again Fiedler's phrase, 'a weariness with the striving to be men', and ponder its implications.

The gulf between morals and aesthetics is not only wider than it has ever been before but many assume that there is no connection whatsoever between them. Susan Sontag, a critic whose perspicacity I admire but whose conclusions I challenge, speaks of Nabokov's *Lolita* as 'the only indisputable "masterpiece", aside from Burroughs' *Naked Lunch*, written in English since World War II', and proceeds to observe that, with the exception of *Pnin*,

> 'all of Nabokov's narratives centre on the consciousness of a deranged person, both sexually obsessed and homicidal'.

---

[1] The following by Camus in *La Vie Intellectuelle* (1949) is illustrative of this attitude: 'Contemporary disbelief no longer relies on science as it did at the end of the last century. It denies both science and religion. It is no longer a sceptical reaction to miracles. *It is passionate disbelief'.* (Italics mine.)

Apparently she does not realise that literature is *affective,* and it is interesting to speculate upon her reactions were a Humbert Humbert to indicate an interest in her own daughter. Yvor Winters gives an illustration of the folly of the lack of such realisation when he writes that, if we consider such writers as Plato, Augustine, Dante, Shakespeare, Rousseau, Voltaire, Emerson, and Hitler, to go no further,

> 'we must be aware that such literature has been directly or indirectly one of the greatest forces in human history. The gospels gave a new direction to half the world; *Mein Kampf* very nearly reversed that direction'.

This absence of a contact with reality is a peculiar characteristic of the intellectual who is essentially a product of the last two centuries. Raskolnikov is, once more, illustrative. His brain is so filled with abstract theories that he has not only lost contact with reality but also with himself; 'A heart unhinged by theories', is the verdict of the prosecuting officer, Porfiry Petrovich. He commits the murder almost in a trance and only afterwards, painfully and inexorably, does he confront his true self and his 'punishment' begins with the realisation of what he has done.

Since such diverse personalities as Matthew Arnold, Jacques Barzun and Eric Hoffer have indicated, to a greater or lesser extent, a distrust of 'intellectualism' translated into the sphere of action, it is perhaps worth pausing to attempt a fresh definition of the term.

I suspect that most readers would feel vaguely uneasy in applying the epithet 'intellectual' to Chaucer, Spenser, Shakespeare, Dryden, Pope, Swift, Fielding, Johnson or Dickens; 'genius' possibly, but not 'intellectual'. I propose now to substitute the term 'Raskolnikovian' for a certain type of 'intellectual', in the hope that a useful distinction can be made between the types of mind exemplified by, let us say, Henry Fielding and Alfred Jarry. Both were writers and both were, using the term loosely, satirists; but there the similarity ends. The former attacked *specific* abuses in his contemporary society: the abuses of power at all levels, the ignorance of country justices, the hypocrisy, the squalor and cruelty of 18th-century London; but his intention was to *reform* society. One feels that Fielding, in his capacity as magistrate, was acquainted at first-hand with the abuses he attacked. He does not lose touch with reality nor does he become absorbed in *abstract* social theorising. In other words, one gets the impression of a man genuinely fascinated by and tolerant of human nature, even when fiercely attacking its weaknesses.

This is the same urbane tolerance that we observed in Mr Bennet's reaction to his wife's interminable follies. And it is this same quality that we find in Chaucer, Spenser, Shakespeare and the other writers cited above. Even the *saeva indignatio* of Swift was not sufficient to prevent him from giving a large percentage of his income to the poor, and his famous remark:

'... all my love is towards individuals. ... Principally, I hate and detest that animal called man, although I heartily love John, Peter, Thomas and so forth',

illustrates not so much his hatred and detestation of man, so much as of abstract, sentimental, blatherers who profess to love mankind as a whole, while in reality pursuing selfish ends. As one example of 'abstract love' for humanity the following by Edward Bond, taken from the Author's Note to the play *Saved*, is typical:

'Clearly the stoning to death of a baby in a London park is a typical English understatement. Compared to the 'strategic' bombing of German towns it is a *negligible atrocity*; compared to the cultural and emotional deprivation of most of our children its consequences are *insignificant*'. (Italics mine.)

Presumably each *individual* Jew's death in the concentration camps was also 'a negligible atrocity'. Burke saw the same selfishness at the root of the abstract theorising of the French Revolutionary leaders:

'Humanity and compassion are ridiculed as the fruits of superstition and ignorance. *Tenderness to individuals is considered as treason to the public*'. (Italics mine.)

The danger inherent in abstract theorising is that sooner or later someone will attempt to put such theories into practice—a Raskolnikov, a Lenin, a Hitler or a Mao Tse-tung. And, if one considers the régimes which these last three have established, each one has been characterised by an utter disregard for individuals, a contempt for tenderness and compassion, all in the name of some high ideal. Arnold foresaw the dangers of the practical application of abstract ideas when he wrote:

'Ideas cannot be too much prized in and for themselves, cannot be too much lived with; but to transport them abruptly into the world of politics and practice, violently to revolutionise this world to their bidding,—that is quite another thing. There is the world of ideas and there is the world of practice'.

In the case of Alfred Jarry, we find in marked contrast to Fielding a savage satire directed against absolutely everything, including the world and the cosmos. It is obvious that, where Fielding's aim was constructive, Jarry's was destructive, even if in the process it involved self-destruction. This is the epitome of the 'Raskolnikovian' temper, and it is well-illustrated in the following description of 'The Harvard aesthetes' (1912-1919), taken from Malcolm Cowley's essay, 'Dos Passos: Poet Against The World', in *After The Genteel Tradition*:

'They [the aesthetes] did not seek to define their attitude except vaguely, in poems; but I think that most of them would have subscribed to the following propositions:

85

That the cultivation and expression of *his* own sensibility are the only justifiable aims for a poet;

That *originality* is his principal virtue;

That society is *hostile, stupid* and *unmanageable*; it is the world of the philistines, *from which it is the poet's duty and privilege to remain aloof;*

That the poet is always misunderstood by the world, and *should, in fact, deliberately make himself misunderstandable,* for the greater glory of art;

That he *triumphs over the world,* at moments, by mystically including it within himself: these are his moments of *ecstasy to be provoked by any means* in his power—*alcohol, drugs, ascetism* or *debauchery, madness, suicide;*

That art, the undying expression of such moments, exists apart from the world; *it is the poet's revenge on society.'* (Italics mine.)

How accurate a representation of the Harvard aesthetes this is, I am not in a position to assess. It is however, an almost perfect description of the 'Raskolnikovian' attitude to art and society. Taking Cowley's propositions one by one, the following deductions may be made.

The 'Raskolnikovian' is dedicated to selfish self-fulfilment (cf., Mailer's statement that 'whether the life is criminal or not, the decision is to develop the psychopath in oneself', or Jimmy Porter's 'I don't care if she's going to have a baby, I don't care if it has two heads', etc.). In order to be successful he must out-shock his competitors (cf., Jarry, Osborne, Genet, Picasso, Albee *et al.*). He is contemptuous of society from which he feels alienated and towards which he exhibits an arrogant disdain. This includes almost the whole *avant-garde* literary movement.

What seems to be ignored by such intellectuals is that the possession of intelligence *per se* is no more cause for pride than physical endowments like brown eyes or fair hair. It is the *direction* in which our intellect is exerted that ought to count. History records endless examples of the evil and destruction wrought by brilliant, unscrupulous knaves and by those who prostituted their talents to serve purely selfish ends.

He must always be obscure; to be easily understood by the masses is to court disaster and earn contemptuous dismissal from 'Raskolnikovian' circles. (If I am accused of misrepresenting the motives of modern writers, I would reply that their motives are unimportant when compared to the effect of their work and if a man deliberately courts obscurity he must expect to be imperfectly understood.) This effect has led to the fragmentation of society, the withdrawal of mimesis to which Toynbee refers and the loss of Unity of Culture which Yeats deplored.

In order to achieve self-fulfilment, or 'self-actualisation', no limit is set upon his behaviour. The sadomasochistic element is apparent in such phrases as 'he *triumphs* over the world', 'the poet's *revenge* on society', and the inclusion of madness and suicide among the permissible means of achieving '*ecstasy*'.

From the foregoing, one dominant fact emerges. The 'Raskolnikovian' temper is destructive, both of self and of society. In this respect it is an unthinkable epithet to apply to the majority of the great writers of the past. Blake is perhaps the first major writer to exhibit some, though by no means all, of the traits enumerated above, and even today there are one or two authors eminent enough to see through the modishness and selfish unconcern for humanity which are exhibited by the 'Raskolnikovians'. Saul Bellow, for example, on the occasion of an award for *Herzog* made it quite explicit that to regard alienation as the sole characteristic of modern man's dilemma and to insist on regarding modern society as 'frightful, brutal, hostile to whatever is pure in the human spirit', is to be guilty of distortion and unnecessary pessimism.

Of prime importance is the fact that the characteristics I have used to define the 'Raskolnikovian' are found not only in a description of the Harvard aesthetes between 1912-1919, but are present to a greater or lesser extent in Dostoevsky's protagonist in *Crime and Punishment,* which was completed in December 1866. The modern 'Raskolnikovian' tends to justify his social and artistic attitudes by referring to the social and moral disintegration of two world wars, the impending horrors of atomic warfare, the dehumanising effects of automation and a computerised society; but the 'Raskolnikovian' mentality ante-dates all these pretexts by at least a century. Just as I have stated that the cumulative effect of Lyell, Darwin, Freud and others does not wholly account for the contemporary lack of religious faith, so I would suggest that world wars, the bomb, and automation are being used, partially at least, as excuses for what in fact is self-indulgence.

The unselfish, cultivated mind attempts to cope with problems in a practical fashion, as in Dryden's *Absolom and Achitophel.* By directing his satire at the English people's restless and fruitless quest for a perfect ruler and a perfect religion ('God's pampered people whom debauched with ease/No King could govern, nor no God could please'), and at the demagogic nature of the Earl of Shaftesbury's activities against Charles II, the poem undoubtedly helped to avert the miseries of a second Civil War. In a modern context, one might opine that Orwell's *1984*, written in clear and forceful prose, has done more to alert 20th-century man to the impending perils of the technological age than all the obscure, self-pitying poems on the subject. 'Evil', wrote Thomas Hood, 'is wrought by want of Thought, as well as want of Heart,' but the 'Raskolnikovian' displays a want of both qualities. Selfishness implies heartlessness, and the hatred and detestation of rationalism precludes thought.

This does *not* mean that there is no room for emotion in human life or that there is no validity in Pascal's statement that 'the heart has its reasons which reason knows nothing of', but to assume that emotion is *all* that is needed, to cultivate it exclusively by any means in one's power including drugs, suicide, and even murder, to deliberately 'develop the psychopath in oneself', and to hold reason and the rational processes in contempt, is to descend to the level of the Yahoo or Trousered Ape.[1]

No work in literature has been so consistently misconstrued as the final book of *Gulliver's Travels*. In fact, Swift is satirising Gulliver's exaggerated respect for the *Houyhnhnms*, who symbolise abstract reason divorced from feeling. Gulliver in his vain pride attempts to become a *Houyhnhnm* and in so doing loses his compassion for his own species. On his return home he is depicted as unable to stand the sight and smell of his wife and children, finding solace only in the company of his horses; a man alienated from society and mentally deranged. The moral is obvious: man should neither aspire to be a God nor descend to the level of the brute. This is the dominant theme of Pope's *Essay on Man* and countless other poems, novels, sermons and philosophical treatises of the period, and until we rediscover a

[1] In his book, *A Sign For Cain*, the psychologist, Fredric Wertham, has the following observation on Norman Mailer's *An American Dream:*

'. . . a man's murder of his wife is presented as a positive act in the development of his personality, as a liberation, a *catharsis*. After the murder, illness passes away from the murderer. This strikes one as a misunderstanding of psychotherapeutic principles'.

Murder as 'therapy' is also evident in a number of contemporary plays, e.g. Arthur Adamov's *Le Sens de la Marche*.

working balance between rationalism and emotionalism the 'Raskolnikovian' destructive element will continue to dominate our literature and art.

Writing of the French critic Antonin Artaud, George Wellwarth, after pointing out that Artaud formulated into a dramatic theory what Jarry had expressed intuitively, writes:

> 'The mere existence of a figure like Ubu, whose heedless freedom makes "civilised behaviour" look ridiculous, is a protest in itself'.

But surely one is at liberty to question this statement. Does Ubu's 'heedless freedom', expressed in greed, cruelty, and an obsession with the animalistic, in reality make 'civilised behaviour' look ridiculous, or is one being impossibly naive in thinking the converse to be true? To assent to Wellwarth's proposition is to invert all values, to infer that greed, cruelty and an obsession with the animalistic are not ridiculous, and implicitly that they are 'better' than altruism, mercy and a suppression of one's animal instincts. Artaud's theories are essentially yet another repudiation of civilisation. They are based upon the assumption that men are naturally barbaric and that culture has corrupted them. Wellwarth wrote:

> 'Only the instinctive desires (anger, hate, longing, the physical desires, etc.) are worthy of consideration by the artist'.

Camus however came to realise that the nihilism and consequent moral vacuum caused by such theories lead to Nazism, Communism and other forms of human tyranny.[1] Far from giving man freedom, such unbridled

---

[1] Erich Fromm in *Escape From Freedom* suggests that the sado-masochistic mind springs from 'the inability to bear the isolation and weakness of one's own self'. He goes on to term the sado-masochist, the *'authoritarian character'* and says that it 'represents the personality structure which is the human basis of Fascism' (and, presumably, any other form of authoritarianism).

licence eventually leads to both self-enslavement and political bondage.

It is precisely because Freud reached the conclusion that the loss of gratification and of sexual freedom is compensated for by the advantages of civilised life that he has been rejected or ignored by so many contemporary writers and artists. As Leslie Fiedler expresses it:

> 'Freud has come to seem too timid, too puritanical and above all too *rational* for the second half of the Twentieth Century . . . It is William Reich who moves the young with his anti-nomianism, his taste for magic and his emphasis on full genitality as the final goal of man'.

In view of what I have already written, any comment on this quotation would be superfluous. I shall leave the reader the task of speculating upon Samuel Johnson's reaction to the concept of 'full genitality as the final goal of man'.

6   The Tyranny of Demos

The lengthened shadow of a man
Is history, said Emerson
Who had not seen the silhouette
Of Sweeney straddled in the sun.

T. S. Eliot:
'Sweeney Among the Nightingales'

Stephen Spender recalls that in 1930 he asked T. S. Eliot what future he foresaw for civilisation. Eliot's reply—'Internecine fighting . . . People killing one another in the streets'—appears, today, to be uncannily prophetic. More recently in *A Sign For Cain*, Dr Fredric Wertham, the American psychologist, has expressed the opinion that mankind is nearer to mass violence than ever before in its history. He observes that such violence is invariably a product of the prevailing social-historical conditions, and that if we look at art historically it is possible in certain epochs to distinguish either an anti-violent or a pro-violent tendency.

Wertham's statistics (though confined to American television) leave little doubt which of these tendencies our age manifests. He has calculated that in a single week one station showed over three hundred completed or attempted killings (mostly during children's viewing time). During the same period the various channels serving a large city displayed almost eight thousand acts of violence. The effect of this, he maintains, is a blunting of sensitivity, and adds that this is not merely an opinion but a clinical fact.

> 'Children have an inborn capacity for sympathy. But that sympathy has to be cultivated . . . And it is this point that the mass media trample on. Even before the natural feelings of compassion have a chance to develop, the fascination of overpowering and hurting others is displayed in endless profusion. Before the soil is prepared for sympathy, the seeds of sadism are planted.'

Wertham denies the comfortable belief that violence can provide a form of *catharsis* and asserts that 'far from providing an innocuous outlet, the brutal and sadistic stories . . . lead natural drives into unhealthy channels'.[1] To substantiate this, he points out that between 1958 and 1965 the crime rate in the United States rose five times faster than the increase in population.

It would be unfair to attribute the phenomenal increase in crime (particularly crime of a violent nature) exclusively to the mass media. On the other hand, if modern Western man is continually subjected to an image of himself as violent, passionate, animalistic and sadistic, not only by the mass media but also in the currently fashionable philosophic treatises, plays, novels and other art forms, it would appear that he can do one of three things. He can react strongly against such representations; he can be unmoved by them; he can consciously or unconsciously mould his own attitude and behaviour to conform with them.

Let us consider these possibilities in turn. Few have the moral courage or social tenacity to espouse the first course, particularly since the terms 'reaction' and 'reactionary' have, under the concentrated attack of 'Raskolnikovians', acquired misleading and pejorative

---

[1] At a recent meeting of the American Psychiatric Association, over 80 per cent of those present agreed with a statement made by Dr Wertham that 'when the environment tolerates violence, violent behaviour is apt to happen'.

connotations in politics, the arts and religion. This is particularly so in the United States where novelty is prized for its own sake ('new' is a holy word in advertising circles), where gentility is suspect as being non-egalitarian, and where there is neither an Established Church, nor a tradition of Burkean Conservatism, to act as brakes on the religious and political organisations.[1]

De Tocqueville foresaw clearly the path which 20th-century literature would take when he wrote:

'The language, the dress, and the daily actions of men in democracies are repugnant to conceptions of the ideal'.

An ideal is, by definition, a concept or standard of supreme perfection, or in human terms, a person of the highest excellence. Egalitarianism, on the contrary, demands a uniform parity of behaviour, and in its most extreme ideological form, even of attainment. Under these conditions the ideal becomes an enemy. No longer is it regarded as a mode of life to be emulated but as a force to be destroyed, since its existence denies (or at least renders questionable), the whole basis of an egalitarian society.

It can now be seen that the distinction which Bate draws between the classical and the naturalistic (to which I referred in the second chapter), is more than a purely literary phenomenon. Neo-classicism, which 'conceives the highest as the norm and regards whatever

[1] Trilling writes as follows in the Preface to *The Liberal Tradition:* 'In the United States at this time, Liberalism is not only the dominant but even the sole intellectual tradition. For it is the plain fact that nowadays there are no conservative or reactionary ideas in general circulation.' If this is true (and I have no reason to doubt Professor Trilling's statement), then far from being a cause for rejoicing, it should be one for public concern. Everyone who has been confronted with a 'simple' problem in his everyday life is well aware that there are two sides to every question. If, as Trilling suggests, the modern intellectual sees only one side (i.e., the liberal), this is yet another example of the *abstract* nature of intellectualism, its divorce from the world of reality.

94

falls below not as "natural" but as corruption', was a product of a hierarchical society.   Contemporary literature, on the other hand, which tends to regard the lowest as the norm is a product of an egalitarian society. It would be difficult to find a clearer example than this of the close relationship which exists between society and its literature, and it is impossible to see any return to an ideal being accomplished while the social and political climate is hostile to any such concept.

Contemporary authors, playwrights and poets thus find themselves in a disconcerting dilemma.   If they attempt to delineate an ideal, they are accused of snobbery, of being anti-proletarian, illiberal, undemocratic and, in certain instances, even racist. Accordingly, all but a dwindling minority have chosen to join the 'Raskolnikovian' ranks of iconoclasts, consoling themselves with the thought that they are allied to 'progress' and apparently forgetting that the Gadarene swine were also 'progressing' as they rushed headlong to destruction.

We turn to the second possibility—that man is unaffected by the books he reads, the plays, films and television programmes he watches.   To accept this would imply a denial of the affective theory of literature, held by Plato, Aristotle, Longinus, Sidney, Johnson, Arnold, Eliot, to name only a few of the leading critics.

Plato, it will be recalled, would have excluded 'the poet' or creative writer from the Republic because of his adverse effect upon the young.   Aristotle's theory of *catharsis*, which has been variously interpreted by commentators, obviously involved the audience being affected by the drama.   Longinus defined a great work of literature as one

> 'which bears a repeated examination, and which it is difficult or rather *impossible to withstand* and the memory of which is strong and hard to efface'.   (Italics mine.)

Sidney's *Apologie For Poetrie* rests largely upon the creative writer's ability to create models of a higher order than nature provides, for men to emulate. Johnson on one occasion asked, 'What is the use of books if they are not to teach us how to live?' Arnold, who defined literature as 'a criticism of life', declared that the best has 'a power of forming, sustaining and delighting us', while Eliot, as has been already shown, was firmly convinced that the reader is profoundly affected by the attitude displayed by an author to his characters.

It would seem, therefore, that of the three alternatives the last is the most likely and that consciously or unconsciously we are influenced by, and tend to emulate, the fictional characters displayed for our edification or entertainment. If this is so, then many contemporary novelists and dramatists appear to be teaching 'bloody instructions, which, being taught, return to plague the inventor'. If McLuhan is right in maintaining that it is possible for whole cultures to be programmed in such a way that their emotional climate becomes stable then the converse may be even more true: that a culture can be whipped up into mass frenzy and violence.

A writer of fiction depends upon the response of the public to his work and, if he ignores this sense of responsibility to that public, he is breaking his part of a social contract. Camus wrote:

> 'We all carry within us our places of exile our crimes and our ravages. But our task is not to unleash them on the world; it is to fight them in ourselves and in others'.

It would appear that in our desire to escape from the rigidity and restraint of the genteel tradition, we have rushed headlong to the other extreme, and have embraced the animalistic and the violent. As an example of this tendency, Louis Kronenberger stated that the most important of H. L. Mencken's contributions to American literature was his struggle 'to purge our literature of its puritanism and gentility'. Consequently, he writes, 'Sex ceased to be a bugaboo, squalor a taboo, decorum a virtue, iconoclasm a subversion of ethics'. 'So far', he adds, 'so good'; but that is just the point. Most of those who originate revolutions, whether in politics, religion or taste, would be appalled were they able to see the extreme to which their theories are extended by subsequent disciples. Sex has not only 'ceased to be a bugaboo', but its perpetual exploitation has made it so monotonous that the portrayal of normal sex has been largely abandoned in favour of the abnormal. Squalor has been elevated to a position of virtue, decorum has become a vice and the subversion of ethics is so taken for granted that anyone who attempts to discuss such a matter is regarded as a cultural peasant or, even worse, a 'reactionary'.

In *Notes et contre-notes*, the playwright Ionesco writes:

> 'I have no other images of the world except those of evanescence and brutality, vanity and rage, nothingness or hideousness, unless hatred. Everything I have since experienced has merely confirmed what I had seen and understood in my childhood: vain and sordid fury, cries suddenly stifled by silence, shadows engulfed forever in the night'.

Is one wrong in thinking this to be an unusually morbid and repellent picture of childhood and in sensing here also a masochistic delight in reliving experiences, coupled with a sadistic desire to make the reader share in the degradation which such a view of life entails? We can recognise the senselessness and evil of much that occurs in human life, without making a religion of that recognition and without assuming that this is all or even a major portion of life. Ionesco's world-view is typically 'Raskolnikovian' and totally antithetical to that which in earlier ages characterised the civilised mind.

Plato maintained (and child psychology largely confirms) that only in rare instances will there be a good man 'who has not from his childhood been used to play amid things of beauty and make of them a joy and a study'. From his writings in general, one may deduce that by 'a good man' he meant an individual who is not a slave to his body, who is capable of appreciating both intellectual and aesthetic beauty and who has sufficient civic pride to play a useful part in society. The very fact that this excludes a large number of people is enough to make it repugnant to an egalitarian culture, but when one examines his statement objectively, it explains many of the problems confronting modern cities and made worse by urban sprawl.

The equation of the city, largely populated by urban peasantry, with cultivated life is possibly the greatest error perpetrated by modern man. It was Thomas Jefferson who wrote: 'I view great cities as pestilential to the morals, the health and the liberties of man'. The urban dweller is induced in a variety of ways to regard the country-man with contempt. This is understandable when one reflects that the vast majority of city-dwellers are *parvenus* in terms of city residence, having moved there in the course of the last two or three generations. Like all *parvenus*, they regard their origins with distaste and attempt to repudiate them. The loss in terms of a rhythmic response to natural life is incalculable, particularly since the majority is unaware of the real cause of its frustrations. Lewis Mumford in *The City In History* shrewdly described the urban dweller as living

'in a self-annihilating moment-to-moment continuum. The poorest Stone Age savage never lived in such a destitute and demoralised community'.

Demos in its hatred of superior beings is essentially destructive and megalopolis is both its symbol and its capital city. Spengler observes that the

'tradition of an old monarchy, of an old aristocracy, of an old polite society . . . insofar as they possess honour, abnegation, discipline and the genuine sense of a great mission, sense of duty and sacrifice—can become a centre which holds together the being stream of an entire people and enables it to outlast this time and make its landfall in the future'.

It is difficult to conceive a greater contrast to such a tradition than the modern megalopolis, 'the unreal city' of *The Waste Land*, filled with millions of alienated strangers, each one pursuing his own aims and ends, selfishly intent upon his own business.

It is not irrelevant, here, to speculate on one other possible result of egalitarianism. Camus maintained that the death of God was followed by the deification of Man; but is it not possible that the reverse is true, and that the deification of man has brought about the death of God? The deity is (or was) the embodiment of the highest ideal known to man, omnipotent, omniscient, the sumpreme *authority* of heaven and earth. Such a concept of a non-elected, superior, authoritative Being is clearly inimical to those who hold extreme egalitarian principles.

The traditional concept enshrined in 'The Great Chain of Being', which envisioned a hierarchical scale descending from God to the angels, and thence to man, brutes and so on, had a social equivalent in the Kings, nobles, yeomen (later the middle-class) and peasantry. It is surely not without significance that the almost total disappearance of Kings and nobility has coincided with the waning of belief in their spiritual counterparts—God and the angels. Although the theory cannot be proved or disproved, the coeval decline of God and royalty is sufficiently striking to merit some such hypothesis.

In fact, the whole question of correspondences remains largely unexplored; William Whewell (the 'Catastrophist'), in his *Philosophy of the Inductive Sciences* (1840), spoke of an historical chain 'which is extended from the beginning of things down to the present time'. The links of this chain he saw as causes of all cosmic events

> 'from those which regulate the imperceptible changes of the remotest nebulae in the heaven, to those which determine the progress of civilisation, polity, and literature'.

More recently Ruth Anshen (editor of the series *World Perspectives*) suggests the possibility that

> 'the creative process in the human mind, the developmental process in organic nature, and the basic laws of the inorganic realm may be but varied expressions of a universal formative process'.

Both these hypotheses provide an explanation for the compact unity which every historical epoch presents. They also imply an historical determinism, a close ally to despair. When man adopts a deterministic attitude to events, he becomes a passive spectator of human destiny, unable to exercise any influence over the forces moulding his thoughts and actions, a victim and not a shaper of history. Under such circumstances, mankind is totally unable to withstand the rise of Nazism or any other form of oppression and even, in the last analysis, to judge, since the inevitability of such régimes makes a mockery of moral judgement. The increasing tendency by novelists and dramatists to depict contemporary man as a victim rather than as a hero, is an indication of the potency and prevalence of such an outlook. Predictably, this coincides with a growing reluctance to judge, a refusal to accept normative standards and an uncritical acceptance of relativism. Ultimately all actions and values, virtue and vice, normalcy and abnormality, truth and falsehood, become meaningless and social, aesthetic and cultural anarchy prevails. The result is a society in which everything is permitted—the final triumph of egalitarianism since all human actions (as well as men) are reduced to a state of unjudgeable equality.

Extreme egalitarianism would appear to be not only the ultimate product of determinism but also, in a cyclical manner, its original source. In a hierarchical society, the mass of people is disposed to feel that the ruler or ruling class is in control of events. They may not approve of the policies being implemented but at least they are being manipulated by a human force. At such times, history is regarded as the outcome of the actions of 'great men', whether they be oppressors or liberators. In an egalitarian society, however, the converse tends to be true. As de Tocqueville has observed:

> 'In the ages of equality all men are independent of each other, isolated and weak. The movements of the multitude are not permanently guided by the will of any individuals: at such times *humanity seems always to advance of itself*'. (Italics mine.)

Much of contemporary despair springs from an absence of absolute standards and of any authority, sacred or secular, and herein lies a curious paradox. Man desires freedom to do as he wishes but, once such a state is attained, sickens of the ensuing moral and social anarchy. The 'Raskolnikovian', characterised by a desire to destroy both himself and society, is frequently not only the instigator of such 'freedom' movements but also the only one who enjoys the outcome. His sadism is gratified by the destruction of order, while he derives masochistic pleasure from the ensuing chaos and purposelessness in which he, together with the rest of humanity, is enveloped.

In *The Rhetoric of Fiction*, Wayne Booth observes that

'one possible reaction to a fragmented society may be to retreat to a private world of values, but another might well be to build works of art that themselves help to mould a new consensus'.

Acknowledging that there are philosophical and psychological obstacles militating against such a consensus, he singles out nihilism as the most powerful of these. Nihilism is after all not merely despair and negation but, above all, the desire to despair and negate. It is necessary to recognise that there is an intellectual and moral fifth column, a cultural guerilla group, at work in literature and society. There is not only 'a weariness with the striving to be men' but an active desire on the part of some for such weariness, an apocalyptic death-urge, that *Weltschmerz* which Well-warth concedes to be the chief philosophical standpoint of the *avant-garde.*

Broadly speaking, literature can be described as aristocratic in tone until approximately 1700; thereafter it became increasingly middle-class until about 1914 when it began to assume a proletarian nature. As Anthony Lejeune has pointed out, much of contemporary literature may be about the common man but it can hardly be intended for him. One suspects that an exclusively proletarian audience would yawn hopelessly through *Waiting for Godot* and at the conclusion demand its money back. Lejeune proceeds to ask if anyone really wants

'a society shaped by John Osborne for the delectation of Jimmy Porter, or plunged into lunacy by Harold Pinter or peopled by the hideous imaginings of Genet or Beckett?'

He concludes that no one (including these writers) would wish to inhabit such a world. While Lejeune emphasises the wide gap between the abstract theoretical world presented to the public by these dramatists and the world of reality, he appears to ignore the mania for iconoclasm which permeates the modern arts, an iconoclasm closely linked to egalitarianism.[1] The only way to ensure complete and absolute equality is to reduce all men to the same level, to deny man's dignity, to stress his animalism and to sneer at any form of idealism.

Confronted by 'The Absurd', Camus saw initially two courses open to man—physical suicide or philosophical suicide. But is it not possible that there is a third form of suicide, what one might term social suicide? Suicide is the result of a ceasing to strive, a desire to cease to be. An ideal, on the other hand, involves a perpetual struggle towards an unreachable goal. This is the distinction Ortega makes between the noble life and the common life.

> 'Nobility is synonymous with a life of effort, ever set on excelling itself, in passing beyond what one is to what one sets up as a duty and an obligation. In this way, the noble life stands opposed to the common or inert life, which reclines statically upon itself, condemned to perpetual immobility, unless an external force compels it to come out of itself.'

Effort is, therefore, incompatible with conscious hedonism; but mass-life with its lack of need for social or spiritual striving (which, theoretically at least, regards any such striving as pretentious and anti-

---

[1] This iconoclasm manifests itself in all art forms and not just in literature. In an article, 'Pop Music Gives Voice To A Restless Generation' (*National Observer*, 15 January, 1968), Daniel Greene writes as follows:

> 'Places long known for high-brow or Hollywood-slick entertainment now vibrate to the cacophony of "psychedelic" and acid-rock; the trenchant strains of folk- and protest-rock; the sensual effusion of "soul"; the raucous incongruity of a new harsh "music" made from an activity as old as mankind: *"destruction—instruments are smashed or blown up"*.' (Italics mine.)

In 1966 a Destruction in Art Symposium was held in London and an invitation to attend was issued to 'all artists who have used *actual destruction of materials* as part of their technique'.

egalitarian) is ideally suited to such pleasure-seeking. The *panem et circenses* philosophy of rulers is not just a cynical interpretation of the desires of the mass, but a realistic evaluation of such. Asceticism, on the other hand, is not likely to appeal to an egalitarian culture because it pre-supposes that some will be more successful than others in achieving such an ideal. Full genitality, however, is an eminently suitable goal for such a culture, since copulation is the common denominator to all, civilised man and savage alike. 'What's the point of a revolution', sings the chorus in Weiss's *Marat-Sade*, 'without general copulation?' What point, indeed, since only when all men are bent solely upon gratifying their physical desires can true equality be imposed. In other words, egalitarian societies are hedonistic both as a result of being egalitarian and as a means of perpetuating and protecting the basis of their existence.

Situational Ethics, which results in every man becoming his own judge and moralist, is but another manifestation of the egalitarian and anti-authoritarian spirit which permeates the modern scene. The violence and animalism which dominate the contemporary arts can now be seen in still another light, though continuing to be part of the compact unity of our epoch. The violence is the fury of the proletarian writer who, not realising (or not wishing to admit) that he is already victorious, continues to fulminate against the old order, against nobility, against gentility, against all 'pretensions', which he styles hypocrisy. To be 'natural' is everything, and is not animalism the most natural state of man? Moreover, in such a state, are not all men equal?[1]

[1] Consider the large and growing number of television programmes involving audience participation in which the sole purpose is to humiliate the contestants and thereby strip them of their dignity.

The compulsive hunt for equality can also be seen in the hatred of form and style which characterises contemporary poetry, art and music. Nietzsche observed that strong natures enjoy their 'finest gaiety' in the constraint of style, while, conversely, it is weak characters 'without power over themselves' who hate such constraint. The traditional poet, artist and musician trained long and arduously for his vocation. One recalls the five years which Milton spent at Horton, the exacting apprenticeship of the Renaissance painters under the tutelage of a 'master' ; and the child, Mozart, practising ceaselessly. Since all cannot indulge in such intensive preparation, art must come down from its pedestal and make itself available to the masses. The result is poetry without the bothersome restraint of form, 'pop' art and 'op' art in which anyone can indulge, and music which is so unprofessional by former standards that an amateur can quickly reproduce a passable rendering. (The names of some of the currently fashionable groups are in themselves revealing. One styles itself 'Group Therapy', another 'The Animals'.) It can all be summed up in the words of a currently popular lyric (in itself an echo of Swinburne's 'Glory to man in the highest ! for man is the master of things'), 'We have no need for a God/Each of us is his own'. Similarly 'we' have no need for great poets, artists and musicians, and art is then reduced to the level of subjective therapy, of no greater importance than a cold bath.

The fact that they receive 'prizes' for their participation renders the spectacle even more depressing. This form of 'entertainment' may well be, as Pamela Hansford Johnson suggests, merely a contemporary 'restoration of the pillory, the stocks and the ducking-stool as spectator sports'. The result is what I have called social suicide, which is perhaps merely a variant of Fiedler's 'weariness with the striving to be men'.

The 'confession' of Picasso referred to in the second chapter is again revealing.

> 'From that moment when art is no longer the food of the superior [*l'aliment des meilleurs*], the artist can exteriorise his talent in new formulae, in all manner of caprices and fantasies, and in all varieties of intellectual charlatanism. People no longer seek either consolation or exaltation in the arts.   Instead they seek the new, the extraordinary, the extravagant, the scandalous.'

To those who may ask is this of any major importance, I would reply as follows. Great art is that which in the past sustained and elevated mankind; it represented a conquest by man over the diverse and bewildering complexities of his own nature and of the world surrounding him; it resulted in 'that clarification of life ... a momentary stay against confusion', which Robert Frost maintained was the true aim and purpose of poetry. Such art involves a prodigious effort and concentration on the part of its creator and demands a cultivated response from its audience. As such it is exclusive, both in terms of those able to create it and those who can appreciate it. It constitutes a minority culture and is therefore to be detested and feared by the majority of contemporary writers and artists with their egalitarian allegiance reinforced by the financial rewards of serving an undiscriminating mass market.

Huckleberry Finn has already been removed from some libraries in the United States because of its alleged racist nature; will *Othello* share its fate, followed by *The Tempest*? Will Demos, in fact, and not Caliban, 'cast out Ariel', and will *Henry V*, which portrays a *King* as a hero, be the next victim? The following by Harold Rosenberger emphasises that what I am suggesting is not fantasy:

> 'If history can make into art what is not now art, it can also unmake what is now art. It is conceivable that Michelangelo,

Vermeer, Goya, Cézanne will someday cease to be art; it is only necessary that . . . an extreme ideology shall sieze power and cast out existing masterpieces as creatures of darkness'.

The purpose of this chapter has been to indicate that an extreme ideology is in the process of siezing power, if indeed it has not already succeeded. The censorship of *Huckleberry Finn* should have produced indignant reactions from all true liberals, but prevailing 'liberalism' is basically illiberal and intolerant of any opposition. It is narrow, morally arrogant and has far more in common with other extremist groups than those who espouse it would care to recognise; and anything it considers anti-liberal must surely merit censorship.[1]

A book was recently published in England with the intriguing title, *Fifty Works of English Literature We Could Do Without.* Among the fifty were the following: *The Faerie Queene, Hamlet, The Pilgrim's Progress, Tom Jones, She Stoops to Conquer, The School for Scandal,* Lamb's *Essays, Pickwick Papers, Wuthering Heights, Tess of the D'Urbervilles, Peter Pan, The Forsyte Saga,* and *Alice in Wonderland.* In American literature (which is gratuitously included), the following could, apparently, be dispensed with: *Huckleberry Finn* (predictably), *The Scarlet Letter, Moby Dick, A Farewell to Arms* and *The Sound and the Fury.* The iconoclasm revealed in this list is obvious and its very extent indicates a passionate ideological motive for the rejection of the works enumerated, all of which demand to a greater or lesser extent a cultivated response on the reader's part. They therefore have no place in the mass culture of today, and it is not difficult to see the title of

[1] A short time ago, I delivered Chapter Four of this book as a paper before a group of university teachers. Afterwards, a young woman of advanced 'liberal' views approached me and said in all seriousness: 'You're advocating censorship; you shouldn't be allowed to publish it'.

the book being changed to include the phrase 'you *will* do without'.

The majority of contemporary writers, artists and critics resemble in many respects a mob. They are all moving in one direction, shouting hysterically and manifesting a tendency towards violence, destruction and anarchy. What other than a mob is this? To oppose it is a lonely task. Some readers may feel that to attack a literary trend, originating with Blake and accelerating almost unchecked until today, is simply intellectual arrogance. But when one regards the spiritual agony and suicidal anarchy which permeate the modern, sensitive mind, is it not possible that both society and literature, which shapes and is shaped by society, are on the wrong track?

In the harsh world of reality the road of excess leads not to the palace of wisdom, but to the psychiatric couch or worse. Few of those who died in Buchenwald or Belsen would have appreciated Eliot's 'curious paradox' that 'it is better to do evil than to do nothing'.

Morality always involves a sentiment of submission, a sense of service and obligation. In other words, it demands the recognition of an authoritative norm, be it secular or religious. The terms submission, service and obligation are all antithetical to the contemporary concept of freedom—freedom to write, paint, compose, act, demonstrate, riot as one pleases. We are in the process of experiencing the agonising results of such 'freedom'.

> 'Art', wrote Camus, 'lives only on the constraints it imposes on itself; it dies of all others. Conversely, if it does not constrain itself, it indulges in ravings and becomes a slave to mere shadows. The freest art and the most rebellious will, therefore, be the most classical'.

The alternative, he suggests, is that artists will become lost in nihilism and sterility.

Precisely the same thing is true of society and of individuals; the greatest contentment may be derived from *service* to an ideal. Not unexpectedly, the 'Raskolnikovian' with his cult of unpleasure rejects such contentment and the ideal which is its source. His hatred of submission, service, obligation and any form of morality are, in effect, the product of his destructive nature. The 'freedom' for which he clamours is merely the freedom to unleash his iconoclastic urges on society and upon himself.

It may be objected that the commitment on the part of so many contemporary writers and artists to idealistic movements, such as civil rights and pacifism, invalidates these charges. Superficially, it might appear to do so, but a closer inspection of the manner in which many of them voice their opinions will confirm the inherent truth of my charges.

Commentators have expressed surprise at the belligerency of 'pacifist' groups and have been naively appalled at the violence which characterises the activities of so many apparently idealistically-motivated organisations. It is not on account of the ideals, however, that many who participate in such movements are drawn to them, but because the movements themselves provide an opportunity for a defiance of authority, an emotional outlet for the repudiation of service.

True altruism is such a rare quality that when one finds a *mass* movement ostensibly advocating it, one should immediately be suspicious and search for its true appeal. The 'Raskolnikovian's' attachment to abstract theorising and his avowed love for *all* mankind are due in part to his inability to love any *single* human being other than himself. Moreover, an impersonal ideal tends to accommodate excess and make it socially more acceptable than it would be in a personal relationship. Jimmy

109

Porter may be an ideal abstract symbol, but he is scarcely an ideal husband.

It is necessary to emphasise that a society can never be greater or better than the individuals who constitute it. Society is, in fact, little more than a collective term for a group of individual human beings. If we really wish to improve it, we must begin with ourselves; we must, in Candide's words, 'cultivate our garden'. As we have seen, this concept is a classical one with its emphasis upon an individual ideal as opposed to a collective one. It involves self-control and restraint, both classical virtues, and so will never enjoy popular support.

In addition, as Orwell's *Animal Farm* suggests, a mass revolt (or revolution) invariably and inexorably ends where it begins; the people rid themselves of one set of masters only to find them replaced by another. In retrospect almost all revolutions are sociologically of negligible importance. It is open to serious doubt whether Soviet policy, both internal and external, differs to any measurable extent from that pursued by the Czars, or that China is any more (or less) imperialist under Mao than it was under the Emperors.[1] The moral of Orwell's book is that a political revolution serves but a minor purpose—it gives the populace a brief holiday, an occasion for an emotional 'blow-out', after which it's back to work as usual. What is appalling about such turbulent upheavals is not how little they accomplish but how little they accomplish in comparison to their cost in human suffering.[2]

[1] The former Jugoslav Communist leader, Milovan Djilas, in an interview reported in the *New York Times* (22 November, 1968), is quoted as saying that he saw 'little difference between Soviet policies today in Eastern Europe and the Eastern Mediterranean and the policies of 19th-century Russian imperialism'.

[2] For a full and dispassionate examination of this problem by an historian, see Crane Brinton's *The Anatomy of Revolution*. The

In *The Rights of Man*, prior to accusing Burke of pitying 'the plumage' and forgetting 'the dying bird', Tom Paine spoke of those killed in France during the Revolution and went on to say that our 'astonishment' at 'so few sacrifices will cease when we reflect that *principles,* and not *persons*, were the meditated objècts of destruction'. True, when Paine wrote this work in 1791 he was unable to foresee the excesses of 1793 and 1794, but in his preference for abstract principles to human life (even one human life), he is in effect giving voice to that most evil of creeds: 'The end justifies the means'. In furtherance of this creed and in the name of some abstract, unattained and indeed unattainable future, more than 5 million Russian *kulaks* were either put to death or deported. Nazism, another abstract mass ideology, claimed some 7 million Jews and 7 million other Europeans killed or deported, quite apart from the war casualties. If religion was formerly the opium of the people, then it would seem that in the last century and a half, politics must be their heroin.

---

following from *The Crisis of Our Age* by the Harvard sociologist, Pitirim Sorokin (who substantiates his statement statistically), is also relevant:

'In the course of human history several thousand revolutions have been launched with a view to establishing a paradise on earth. And they are still proceeding at full blast, in spite of the fact that practically none of them has ever achieved its purpose . . . And we observe "Homo sapiens" still engrossed in this crazy quest. From this standpoint, the history of human progress is indeed a history of incurable human stupidity!'

While from a literary standpoint, Milton's sonnet 'I did but prompt the age to quit their clogs' expresses the ageing poet's tragic realisation that the basic infirmities of human nature have made his youthful utopian and revolutionary vision merely an impossible dream:

Licence they mean when they cry liberty;
For who loves that, must first be wise and good;
But from that mark how far they rove we see
For all this waste of wealth and loss of blood.

The material benefits the instigators claim as the fruits of revolution are almost invariably the products of industrialism and technology and would become available to the people regardless of the prevailing political ideology. Such reflections make it all the more incomprehensible that men of the intellectual stature of Sartre can regard commitment to a mass movement such as Communism with any degree of seriousness. The truth is that whereas mass movements inevitably lead to state control, true freedom can only be preserved through an individual ideal based upon self-control.

Furthermore, no measurable improvement can take place in the *spiritual quality* of society until such a personal ideal is recovered, and the fact that such an ideal tends to be aristocratic rather than egalitarian is of minor significance. The great crisis of the present is so urgent and compelling that such considerations are trivial in comparison.

What confronts mankind, white and coloured, republican and royalist, fascist and communist, is no less than the possible decline and fall of man, the self-extermination of the species. In the face of such a challenge, there is a profound need for individuals of high purpose and resolve. Egalitarians insist that all keep in step, artistically, ethically, morally and intellectually. Such a course is suicidal in an age recently described as one of nuclear giants and moral pygmies.

Technologically, where it is of comparatively minor importance, we refuse to take a retrogressive step. Culturally, morally, socially and in terms of our ideals, we betray a suicidal tendency to do so, and if we continue in our present course the gap between our technological potency and ethical impotency will widen into a vast and unbridgeable chasm. The ultimate results of such an attitude, involving the total destruction of self and all society including everything that has been thought, fashioned and striven for by man—the *Agamemnon*, the works of Homer, Virgil, Dante, Shakespeare, Goethe and Tolstoy ; the teachings of Buddha, Confucius, Socrates, Plato, Aristotle, Christ, Augustine, Pascal and Montaigne ; the discoveries of Galileo, Bacon, Locke, Newton, Pasteur, Curie, Einstein and Fleming—will be the ultimate and empty triumph of the 'Raskolnikovian'.

7 Instinctive Morality

'Standards are imaginary things, and yet it is extremely doubtful if man can live well, either spiritually or physically, without the belief that they are somehow real. Without them society lapses into anarchy and the individual becomes aware of an intolerable disharmony between himself and the universe. Instinctively and emotionally he is an ethical animal.'

Joseph Wood Krutch: *The Modern Temper*

Before proceeding further, an investigation into the sources of the theory of an 'absurd' universe is necessary since much of contemporary thought is the direct or indirect result of such a cosmic view. The modern *avant-garde* sees 'The Absurd' as an end in itself, a negation which it is impossible to negate, a spiritual and intellectual *cul de sac* from which there is no exit. For Albert Camus, however, it was essentially a beginning. The absurdity of life, he felt, had to be recognised and confronted by every sensitive, thinking being and must then be overcome. In his speech of acceptance on receiving the Nobel Prize, he opposed 'the mistaken attitude of those who, through excess of despair . . . have rushed headlong into the nihilism of our day'. At the same time he insisted on repudiating the consolations of what he considered the illusions of religion. His attitude may remind one of Hardy's remark: 'If way to the Better there be, it exacts a full look at the Worst'.

In *The Myth of Sisyphus* (1942) Camus declares:

'The perception of an angel or a god has no meaning for me. That geometrical spot where divine reason ratifies mine will always be incomprehensible to me . . . it means for me *forgetting just what I do not want to forget*'. (Italics mine.)

The same essay opens with the challenging and uncompromising statement that there is 'but one truly serious philosophical problem and that is suicide'. This is followed by the bleak sentence: 'Beginning to think is beginning to be undermined', and leads Camus to the overwhelming question: 'Does the Absurd dictate death?'

When Camus wrote this he was too innocent to recognise the dangers inherent in philosophy attenuating itself until it becomes a mere game. Later he came to the conclusion that only a short step separates Nietzsche from Nazism and was to write in *The Rebel:* 'There are crimes of passion and crimes of logic'. In the same essay he is more specific about the nature of such crimes of logic:

'Philosophy secularises the ideal. But tyrants appear who soon secularise the philosophies that give them the right to do so'.

The danger of abstract philosophical speculation (epitomised by Schopenhauer extolling the virtues of suicide while seated at a well-set table, cracking nuts and drinking wine), and of abstract literary theory and practice have already been discussed.

Let us now examine Camus' reasons for espousing 'The Absurd', bearing in mind that he stressed that his attitude towards the subject was provisional and was not to be taken as necessarily his final view. There are, it would appear, five possible sources from which a realisation of the absurdity of life may arise. Firstly, it can emerge from a sudden appreciation of the pointlessness and futility of our daily activities:

'Rising, streetcar, four hours in the office or the factory, meal, streetcar, four hours of work, meal, sleep and Monday Tuesday Wednesday Thursday Friday and Saturday according to the same rhythm . . . But one day the "why" arises and everything begins in that weariness tinged with amazement'.

He admits that there is nothing original in these observations and in fact they are, in essence, a restatement of views held by many earlier writers. Eliot's *Prufrock*, for example, states :

. . . I have known them all already, known them all :
Have known the evenings, mornings, afternoons,
I have measured out my life with coffee spoons . . .

It is significant, however, that both the Eliot of *Prufrock* and Camus are at complete variance with the thought expressed by John Keble in a hymn written in 1822 :

The trivial round, the common task,
Will furnish all we ought to ask ;
Room to deny ourselves—a road
To bring us daily nearer God.

The two attitudes displayed here are yet another manifestation of the swing from self-denial to self-fulfilment which I see as the dominant trend of our age. They also reflect the dilemma of contemporary life—a life which may be described as having tempo but no rhythm. The simple agrarian life which was the lot of the majority in Keble's time, whatever its limitations in economic, social and educational terms, provided a seasonal rhythm and an obvious justification for itself in the raising of food for the family and the community, which modern industrial life symbolised by the conveyor belt appears incapable of providing for all but the totally unimaginative and insensitive.

The second source of the realisation of 'The Absurd' arises when we cease to live in the future and face the 'now' of our existence :

'A day comes when a man notices or says that he is thirty. Thus he asserts his youth. But simultaneously he situates himself in relation to time. . . . He admits that he stands at a certain point on a curve that he acknowledges having to travel to its end. He belongs to time'.

Again, the lack of originality in no way detracts from the truth of Camus' statement. Writers such as Catullus, Marvell, Herrick Donne and, in our own time, Heidegger and Dylan Thomas have all expressed the same horror at the conquering hand of time and the inevitability of death.

The tragedy of man is that intellectually he is aware of the relentless passage of time and yet is impotent to affect its course in any way. The coach rolls on, some stoically accepting the fact, others screaming hysterically, still others stifling the knowledge in drink or drugs or sex, while a dwindling minority continues to nurse a hope that at their journey's end they will find the green sward of eternal consolation. Camus rejected the last two of these attitudes (conscious hedonism and traditional religion) and embraced the stoical approach —'the heart-rending and marvellous wager of the absurd' as he termed it.

The third source of 'The Absurd', according to Camus, lies in man's sense of alienation from the external, natural world:

'At the heart of all beauty lies something inhuman, and these hills, the softness of the sky, the outline of these trees at this very minute lose the illusory meaning with which we had clothed them, henceforth more remote than a lost paradise . . . that denseness and that strangeness of the world is the absurd'.

This might appear to be merely a restatement of Wordsworth's

But yet I know, where'er I go
That there hath passed away a glory from the earth, a statement which is followed by the agonising questions:

Whither is fled the visionary gleam?
Where is it now the glory and the dream?

117

However, a look at the full title of Wordsworth's poem, *Ode: Intimations of Immortality from Recollections of Early Childhood*, reveals a profound and unbridgeable gap between the poet and Camus. Wordsworth, in a naively pre-Freudian fashion, is persuaded that the child's vision of the world is conditioned by his recent emergence from heaven; 'trailing clouds of glory', the child sees this world through the eyes of a heavenly visitant. Soon this vision becomes less intense and the earth loses its splendour and glory which are not innate in it but are rather a reflection of the splendour and the glory of the child's fresh, unblunted, sensibilities. The poem concludes, however, on an optimistic note with Wordsworth consoling himself for his sense of alienation from the natural, external world with the thought that, since he once knew immortality before this life (a fact of which he is persuaded by his memories of childhood), he is therefore guaranteed a return to a similar immortal existence after death. This is yet another example of the determination of 'romantics', almost in spite of themselves, to make sense of the world.

It would appear that the first three sources of 'The Absurd' which Camus propounds are common to most sensitive, thoughtful persons and can, therefore, be deemed to possess a certain validity. The fourth, however, seems arbitrary and suggests that Camus is determined to espouse 'The Absurd', even if he obtains it with a zeal which itself borders upon the absurd:

> 'At certain moments of lucidity', he writes, 'the mechanical aspect of their [men's] gestures, their meaningless pantomime makes silly everything that surrounds them. A man is talking on the telephone behind a glass partition; you cannot hear him, but you see his incomprehensible dumb show: you wonder why he is alive . . . this incalculable tumble before the image of what we are, this "nausea" . . . is also the absurd'.

Now surely there is an illogicality here. 'Moments of

lucidity' cannot co-exist with an artificial stifling of one of the senses (in this case, hearing). One has only to imagine that the inaudible telephone-user is summoning assistance for a wife in labour to see that the absurdity is in the mind of the observer and not in the 'pantomime' of the observed, whose actions may be far from 'mean-ingless'. Recalling the notoriously erroneous descrip-tions of an elephant given by the three blind men, would Camus term their findings the result of 'moments of lucidity' or would he concede them to be totally false?

After his examination of the sources of 'The Absurd' (the fifth, death, is really an elaboration of the second), Camus does admit that in judging the world 'absurd' he has been too hasty: 'The absurd is not in man . . . nor in the world, but in their presence together'. This is, perhaps, the most important statement in *Sisyphus* and provides us with a clue to a possible means of escape from the intellectual impasse which an acceptance of an absurd world imposes.

In his *Essay On Man*, having confronted the same apparent unintelligibility of the cosmos, Pope, under the influence of Newtonian physics, declared the uni-verse to be 'a mighty maze! but not without a plan', and placed the inability to understand the *infinite* in the *finite* mind of man ('Tis but a part we see, and not a whole'). Here we have yet another major difference between the neo-classical outlook and our own: modern man is no longer so easily persuaded that his mind is finite. His scientific and technological progress have been so astonishingly rapid that he cannot readily admit that there are areas of human endeavour, such as metaphysics, theology and philosophy, which remain at best speculative.

Does religious faith entail, as Camus supposes, the sacrifice required by St Ignatius Loyola: 'The sacrifice of the intellect'? Let us profit from Camus' error in supposing that 'moments of lucidity' can co-exist with a deliberate stifling of one of the human senses, and let us imagine a large group of deaf people attempting to listen to and understand a lecturer without the help of lip-reading or a hearing aid. Despite the fact that they may feel a 'wild longing for clarity', the words of the lecturer, no matter how brilliant and lucid he may be, will be totally unintelligible to this particular audience. Is it not more probable that man is similarly devoid of some necessary, additional sixth sense, the lack of which precludes an understanding of the purpose of the universe and of life, than that these phenomena are totally and frivolously devoid of any meaning?

The absurdity in Camus' fourth example lay not in the object observed but in the inability of the observer to understand what he was witnessing because of a situational deficiency. Man, according to Pope, is only 'a being *darkly wise*', and this is an essential belief in both Classical and Hebraic thought. Plato declared that God, as ideal Being, and not man is the measure of all things; and when the Lord out of the whirlwind rebuked Job, it was in terms that stressed man's presumption at attempting to understand His *infinite* purpose:

> Where wast thou when I laid the foundations of the earth? declare, if thou hast understanding.
> Who hath laid the measures thereof, if thou knowest? or who hath stretched the line upon it?

So long as these questions remain unanswered some words of Pascal will remain relevant:

> 'To be mistaken in believing that the Christian religion is true is no great loss to anyone; but how dreadful to be mistaken in believing it to be false!'

A cat or other domestic pet may be induced to focus

120

its eyes upon a newspaper picture of other cats, a mirror, or upon some object which might reasonably be expected to arouse its interest. The result is invariably disappointing. The cat may look at the picture but it obviously does not 'see' it in a human sense. It exhibits no interest whatsoever. Does this mean the picture has no message, that it is meaningless and absurd, or is it not simply that the cat is physically incapable of finding any meaning in it because of some innate deficiency in its sensory apparatus? And may not man be similarly myopic when he contemplates the cosmos, yet through pride refuse to admit this possibility?

Alternatively, it is possible that the vital, sixth sense which would enable man to view life and the universe as intelligible phenomena is not missing but is simply the much-abused and neglected 'instinctive view' of existence. The question 'Does the Absurd dictate Death?' has possibly less immediate relevance than the question 'Does the Absurd dictate that one must live an absurd life, purposeless, unjudgeable, amoral?'. Theoretically, it would seem as though it must, except that man instinctively rebels against such a concept of futility. Certainly in Camus' case, whenever logic collided with his instinctive morality, it was always logic that was jettisoned. In spite of his logic of the absurd, he was unable to put the quisling or the informer on a level with the Resistance fighter; but why? It was this and similar questions which forced Camus to a re-examination of the logical processes leading him to 'The Absurd' and as a result to an eventual rejection of 'Sartrean' existentialism.

In 1944, in the fourth of his *Lettres à un ami allemand,* he wrote:

'You never believed in the meaning of this world and you therefore deduced the idea that everything was equivalent and

> that good and evil could be defined according to one's wishes. You supposed that in the absence of any human or divine code the only values were those of the animal world—in other words, violence and cunning . . . And, to tell the truth, I, believing I thought as you did, saw no valid argument to answer you except a fierce love of justice which, after all, seemed to me as unreasonable as the most sudden passion'.

He proceeds to say that he continues to believe that this world has no ultimate meaning. 'But I know that something in it has meaning and that is man, because he is the only creature to insist on having one'. The illogicality of this dictum (as though by 'insisting' that black is white one can alter the truth of the converse an iota) merely demonstrates that 'the instinctive moralist' is still philosophically at war with himself.

Faced then with his awareness of 'The Absurd', Camus returns to his original question: 'Is one to die voluntarily or to hope in spite of everything?' These two possible reactions to an absurd world he styles respectively physical suicide and philosophical suicide, and deals with the latter first. He rejects the Kierkegaardian 'leap of faith', maintaining that it implies the 'sacrifice of the intellect' and that 'to an absurd mind reason is useless and there is nothing beyond reason'. His attitude to faith at this juncture is uncompromising: 'Seeking what is true is not seeking what is desirable'; and he goes on to state that there can be only two certainties: 'My appetite for the absolute and for unity and the impossibility of reducing the world to a rational and reasonable principle'. These, he feels, are irreconcilable and asks what other hope he can admit without lying, without bringing in a hope which he lacks.

Having rejected philosophical suicide, Camus proceeds to contemplate physical suicide which he also repudiates because to kill oneself voluntarily is to enter into a collusion with death, which is one of the basic sources of an awareness of 'The Absurd'; in other words, physical suicide would be a form of collaboration with the enemy. The rejection of these two possible alternatives would appear to leave Camus where he started, in a philosophic vacuum. But there is something instinctive in him which transcends his logic, a will to negate the negation, and nowhere is this more apparent than in *The Myth of Sisyphus* when, quite illogically, he creates from 'The Absurd' a positive springboard to action :

> 'Is one . . . going to take up the heartrending and marvellous wager of the absurd? Let's make a final effort in this regard and draw all our conclusions. The body, affection, creation, action, human nobility will then resume their places in this mad world. At last man will again find there the wine of the absurd and the bread of indifference on which he feeds his greatness'.

Reading this, one can only say that Camus impresses us more as a moralist than as a logician, a statement justified when we examine his attitude to virtue in the context of his philosophy of 'The Absurd'. 'One can', he writes, 'be virtuous through a whim', but this position is clearly unsatisfactory as a basis for human morality. One can equally well liquidate 8 million Jews through a whim, betray one's comrades to the enemy, impose a totalitarian régime, commit any form of atrocity through a whim, and this is simply the road to amorality and nihilism. If morality is dependent upon a whim, then it can shift and change from day to day and even from second to second. It is surely significant that Camus did not apply the moral and social implications of 'The Absurd' to his own daily life, and here one may draw a useful comparison between his and the 'Raskolnikovian' mentality, exemplified in its extreme form by Jarry. The latter also recognised the absurdity of life but, a victim of abstract intellectualism, attempted

123

and, indeed, succeeded in modelling his own life upon the incoherence and chaos which he believed surrounded him. Camus confronts the same sources of incoherence and despair, but stoically declines to capitulate to them.

The question that cannot remain unasked, however, is why does Jarry's decision seem more consistent, more logical, than Camus'? In other words, *is* there an honest way out of the impasse, or must Ivan Karamazov's reaction to the absence of a God—'Everything is permitted'—continue to dominate and eventually destroy man's aspirations and reduce humanity to the ethics of the Nazi concentration camps? If this question cannot be satisfactorily answered, then nothing but social lethargy and dwindling pockets of residual, orthodox religion and religious morality separate us from lapsing back into jungle-law based upon 'the will to power'.

Let us see if we can attempt, at least, to answer the question positively without the sacrifice of intellectual honesty. It is safe to assume that when the creature destined to become man struggled from the ooze and slime onto dry land, it was obeying some deep instinctive drive. Because of the vagueness and consequent confusion surrounding the term 'instinctive', one might substitute the expression primordial affirmative for this drive. It was this primordial affirmative, the unthinking, unreasoning will to exist, that enabled this ancestral creature to survive and adapt to the varying situations which confronted it during the succeeding millions of years until finally it evolved into a creature recognisable as man. During the whole of this long-drawn evolutionary process, the power of conceptual thought did not exist. The primordial affirmative was sufficiently potent to ensure survival. The possession of conceptual ability is, in fact, a very recent acquisition in man's history, although this is not to suggest that it is unnatural, 'anti-instinctive', artificial, or that it works against the primordial affirmative. On the contrary, it is a perfectly natural refinement and extension of such affirmative or instinctive faculty, shaping, guiding, and preserving life. And if we pause for a moment, we shall see that it could not possibly be otherwise. After all, if this ancestral creature, obeying solely the will to survive, following the dictates of the primordial affirmative, developed voluntarily a method of conceptual thought, then such method could not possibly be alien to it, could not be anything other than a natural outgrowth springing from the creature's own consciousness. One of the greatest fallacies of Western thought has been that the instinctive and the rational faculties are mutually hostile and exclusive. Plato conceived them as dichotomous, as body and mind, and subsequent philosophy and theology have wrangled over the rival claims of these two phenomena which, Freud notwithstanding, are in reality complementary.

Our error lies in not realising which problems to assign to the rational faculty and which to the instinctive. In ordinary, every-day living we experience no difficulty with this problem. In a restaurant a person examines the bill, possibly checks it to ensure that it is correct, calculates a reasonable tip to leave and tenders his money. All this he has rightly assigned to his rational faculties, which have been trained to perform such tasks efficiently. Simultaneously, he is also performing a number of other functions, breathing, hearing, blinking and so forth, automatically and without exercising the discriminating, volitional faculty.

Unfortunately, in the realm of abstract, speculative thought, we are not so competent in what we render to the rational and what to the instinctive. As examples one might cite questions as to the purpose of life, speculation regarding the existence of God, or the existence of right and wrong. To treat the last of these first, if any reader can honestly *feel* that the gas-ovens at Buchenwald were neither right nor wrong, then he is a true relativist. If, on the other hand, he regards such things as *innately* evil then, despite the modishness of contemporary ethical relativism, he is still a member of the human race, even if he cannot *rationally* explain why he feels such things to be evil. Similarly, questions as to the purpose of life, involving the innate will to survive (the primordial affirmative), cannot be rationally considered or answered. Much the same is true of theological belief and controversy. A rational argument between an atheist and a believer is an essay in futility because both are addressing their finite, rational faculties to a problem outside the scope of such faculties. The existence of God can neither be proved nor disproved on rational grounds, and belief involves not so much 'the sacrifice of the intellect' (which, I am suggesting, is incompetent in this matter), but rather the substitution of instinct.

The universe, and this world, may or may not be absurd. Contemporary science appears to indicate a random and therefore 'absurd' cosmos; but when one considers the exploded scientific theories of even a few decades ago, it is surely an unwarranted presumption and an example of crass temporal provincialism to assume that the current scientific view is final and immutable. Faced with such an enigma, it is worth pausing before jettisoning not only the traditional concept of a deity but also the whole moral and ethical fabric, together with the two thousand years of human wisdom woven into our Judeo-Christian tradition, particularly since there appears to be no viable, alternative system of belief to command a general allegiance. Not only does rationalism have its limitations, but what we are in danger of denying or ignoring today is that the same is true of our instincts. They were perhaps all-sufficient for pre-historic man ; but for his contemporary counterpart amid the complexities of the modern world, to attempt to live *solely* by obeying instincts or the dictates of passion is to court disaster and descend to the level of the trousered ape. Contemporary music, art, literature, and drama, with their emphasis upon the primitive and the unregenerate, may be seen as a reaction to the ultra-rationalistic, computerised society, envisioned by such anti-Utopian writers as Aldous Huxley and Orwell. But the *extremism* of such reaction makes it repugnant to the true humanist who wants man neither to become a machine nor to lapse into barbarism. The 18th century possibly over-emphasised the rational. Reacting in what is regarded as an inevitable swing of the pendulum, the 'romantics' over-emphasised the instinctive and the intuitive. What is needed today is a fusion of emotion and intellect ; otherwise we may find ourselves at the mercy of those like Arthur Koestler who in *The Ghost in the Machine* suggests the need for some kind of brain pill to allow the thinking part of the brain to assert constant control over the emotional.

Man has progressed because of the obstacles which he has had to overcome. If life were to come to resemble what geologists refer to as a peneplain (a flat, feature-less landscape), then the consequent inertia and *ennui* would undoubtedly result in entropy. Here then is a major problem of the great crisis of the present, and it can be expressed as follows. Can man continue to exist without forfeiting much of what he now regards as 'human nature'. Moreover, if his desires and passions are controlled by some external and, almost inevitably, authoritarian means, is he doomed to slow decay or extermination?

Neither of these prospects is alluring and in the face of such a choice the sensitive mind might well sink into the quietism of despair. It may be recalled that in the fourth book of *Gulliver's Travels*, Gulliver was faced with the apparent choice of emulating the Houyhnhnms, symbols of abstract dehumanised reason, or degenerating into the bestial state epitomised by the Yahoos. Both alternatives were equally obnoxious to one such as Swift who was brought up in the classical humanist tradition, and Gulliver, infatuated with the horses and neighing instead of speaking, is mercilessly satirised for his failure to espouse a *via media* and continue to be a Man.

The classical and Christian traditions have both emphasised pride and self-love as the chief source of man's sin, whilst indicating that they are but exaggerations of the constructive virtues of dignity and self-respect. In other words, even a virtue ceases to be such if it is carried to *excess*. Today we are confronted with excess on all sides: excessive worship of technology and its dubious fruits; excessive passions and violence in our literature, on the stage, and in our streets. The voice of moderation, reason and restraint recedes into almost total silence. 'The best' appear to 'lack all conviction, while the worst are full of passionate intensity'. Writing of the time prior to the Second World War, when the Nazis had seized power and the remainder of Europe seemed powerless to resist their philosophy of conquest, Camus wrote:

> 'Everywhere philosophies of instinct were dominant and, along with them, the spurious romanticism that prefers feeling to understanding as if the two could be separated'.

'Romanticism', with its emphasis upon supra-individualism, inevitably results in relativism since if all people follow their impulses a wide disparity of both judgements and actions must emerge. Although such relativism may appeal to the youthful, it palls on the adult mind which tires of the ensuing moral and social chaos. Moreover, relativism, which in theory at least disregards social, aesthetic, cultural and ethical norms, is obviously only a step away from the nihilism Camus saw as one of the 'crimes of logic'.

Let us attempt now to pull certain strands together. Spengler saw 'romanticism' as a nostalgic look to the past, to childhood, a step on the way to wishing one-self 'back in the darkness of proto-mysticism, in the womb of the mother, in the grave'. Today's ultra-romantic, *avant-garde* would seem, in their 'death-oriented hopelessness', to lend credence to Spengler's theory. On the other hand, a purely rational society, reasoning all purpose out of life, cannot logically deny that Jarry's deliberate suicide was consistent with its own cosmic view. In other words, exclusive and excessive emotionalism or exclusive and excessive rationalism lead to the same nihilistic terminus. A synthesis of emotionalism and rationalism would seem, therefore, to be the sole hope remaining to man.

Here then is the task which confronts us in the arts and in life. To extol beauty, dignity and grandeur, both in man and nature, is not an escape from realism or from what is natural. There is nothing fundamentally more realistic or more 'natural' about a public urinal, or a kitchen-sink, or a paranoid-schizophrenic than there is about a tranquil lawn, or a cultivated household, or a balanced mind. All exist in this world, and a writer who concentrates exclusively upon the sordid and repellent aspects of life, implying that these are all, is as guilty of distortion as the authors of mawkishly sentimental novelettes.

Writing of man, Robert Louis Stevenson made the following observations in *Pulvis et Umbra* :

'Poor soul, here for so little, cast among so many hardships, filled with so many desires so incommensurate and so inconsistent, savagely surrounded, savagely descended, irremediably condemned to prey upon his fellow-lives; who would have blamed him had he been a piece with his destiny and a being merely barbarous ? And we look and behold him instead filled with imperfect virtues ; infinitely childish, often admirably valiant, often touchingly kind; sitting down, amidst his momentary life, to debate of right and wrong and the attributes of the deity ; rising up to do battle for an egg or for an idea ... To touch the heart of his mystery, we find in him one thought, strange to the point of lunacy ; the thought of duty ; the thought of something owing to himself, to his neighbour, to his God ; an ideal of decency, to which he would rise if it were possible ; a limit of shame below which, if it be possible, he will not stoop ... Of all earth's meteors, here at least is the most strange and consoling ; that this ennobled lemur, this hair crowned bubble of the dust, this inheritor of a few years and sorrow, should yet deny himself his rare delights, and add to his frequent pains and live for an ideal. . . .'

Those who today stress man's animalism, who see him as merely a 'walking bag of sea water', are denying or ignoring that unlike other animals, as Stevenson points out, man *has* striven for a moral order, *has* bridled his own lusts and appetites, *has* tried however pitifully and inadequately to achieve an ideal, *has* created a *Tao* which, as Kluckhohn has pointed out, embraces moral codes that extend beyond what are necessary for mere survival. If such codes fulfil an innate instinctive need, then no amount of intellectual or rational casuistry or sophistry can deny them, since they are not susceptible to debate by the intellectual or rational faculties. If particular virtues have been extolled, certain objects have commanded aesthetic allegiance, and certain ways of life have been recognised as innately good by civilised man for thousands of years, it can only be because such virtues, objects and ways of life have satisfied an imperative need in him. To argue the need, intellectually or rationally, is as absurd as to indulge in rational debate about one's preference for a particular colour, or one's choice of a wife. If we accept such things as innate, as an out-growth of the primordial affirmative, then the intellect is freed to concentrate upon those matters that are its rightful preserve : the problem of world-population ; the question whether we wish to inhabit a world in which man has a place or whether we will allow ourselves to be dominated and eventually outlawed from the natural world by our technocratic skills ; the question whether we want to remain free men or be transformed into semi-slaves or worse of the state. These and allied problems are within the scope of our intellectual capacities, and it is to these increasingly urgent problems that we should address our intellects.

Some will, of course, see this hope as futile and sentimental wishful-thinking. They will point to Buchenwald and Hiroshima as examples of the essential depravity of man and the consequent dis-honesty of any view which presents him in another light. Such fatalism, however, ignores the fact that the concentration camps and the bomb aroused widespread horror in the minds of civilised men throughout the world. Complete hopelessness would be permissible only if there had been a total absence of such reaction, if all mankind had docilely and meekly submitted to the historical expediency of such atrocities and had sought facile relief in degrading justification of the events. That they did not do so is an indication that man still has within him, however battered and bruised, an ideal of what he should be and what human life should be like.

8 To Be or Not to Be

... And he, shall he,
Man, her last work, who seem'd so fair,
Such splendid purpose in his eyes,
Who roll'd the psalm to wintry skies
Who built him fanes of fruitless prayer ...

Who loved, who suffer'd countless ills,
Who battled for the True, the Just,
Be blown about the desert dust,
Or seal'd within the iron hills?

Tennyson: *In Memoriam*

One of the fashionable fallacies, widely prevalent today, is that the problems confronting mankind in the latter half of the 20th century differ only in degree from those faced by previous generations. They are, on the contrary, totally unprecedented and, until this is generally realised and accepted, no move towards their solution will be possible. The sources of the contemporary crisis can be summarised as: an almost total loss of religious faith—a denial of any ultimate reference; a majority of the world's peoples under the age of twenty-five; a population explosion which threatens to engulf mankind; and finally a nuclear ability to destroy the species. Having discussed the loss of religious faith and its consequences, I am now primarily concerned with the problems posed by a predominantly youthful culture and by world over-population.

132

In his *Essay on Criticism*, published in 1711, Pope wrote :

We think our fathers fools, so wise we grow ;
Our wiser sons, no doubt, will think us so.

These lines should dispel any illusions that youthful rebellion is a peculiarly modern phenomenon. Conflict and tension between youth and its elders has always existed and, once the formerly youthful attain maturity and parenthood, they in turn are subjected to the same contempt which they so recently lavished upon their parents. In the past, when the young constituted a powerless minority, this cyclical pattern was of minor importance. Today it is of the utmost significance and constitutes an awesome problem for teachers, psychologists, sociologists and all who are seriously interested in the contemporary scene. As Louis E. Reik, a psychiatrist at Princeton University, has stated,

'the problem of whether the [youthful] individual's aggressive energies will be expressed in useful or destructive ways has never before cast such a deep and terrible shadow over human life'.

In statistical terms, for the first time in the country's history a large proportion of the population of the United States, and of many European countries, is under the age of twenty-five, and this has already had profound political, social, artistic and economic repercussions. Youth has many admirable qualities, including vigour, enthusiasm, a zest for living, and courage. Adults are, however, in danger of forgetting that it is the physical and not the mental attributes of the young which arouse admiration and that as a rule youth does not have, indeed cannot have, those two qualities which more than ever are needed to ensure man's survival— wisdom and restraint. It is surely more than coincidental that the popular appeal of existential philosophy, which

133

places such emphasis on action as opposed to speculation, should have ante-dated a youthful culture by some twenty years?[1] Indeed, action is the dominant cry of today's youth and the political implications constitute a grave threat to civilisation.[2]

It may be recalled that in *Animal Farm*, when the animals' rebellion proved successful and the drunken inefficient Farmer Jones had been forcibly expelled, two pigs, Napoleon and Snowball, vied with each other for control of the farm and its animal occupants. That Napoleon succeeded was due to his indoctrination of some young puppies in whom he was able to inculcate absolute and slavish obedience. No one who is old enough to remember the Hitler Youth or who saw Mao's Red Guards in action can fail to appreciate Orwell's message that youth can be trained, indoctrinated and manipulated by irresponsible politicians and others to further purely selfish ambitions. The ultimate example of this must be the Red Guard which hunted down and

[1] Sartre, defending existentialism against the charge that it induces people to dwell in the quietism of despair, declares that if this were true it would be merely a 'contemplative philosophy'. He goes on to observe that 'since contemplation is a luxury, this would be only another bourgeois philosophy'. In other words 'contemplation' is 'bourgeois' (and anyone versed in Communist jargon is aware that this is equivalent to declaring that contemplation is effete and ignoble). Conversely, one is meant to assume that action is anti-bourgeois (i.e., virile and praiseworthy).

[2] A recent United Nations survey of the world-wide student demonstrations concludes that sit-ins, marches and brawls with the police are only the fore-runner of bigger and bolder protests. World opinion, it predicts, is going to become increasingly the opinion of world's youth and the generation conflict will assume proportions not previously imagined. (The suggestion by Jerry Rubin, the American Yippie leader, to a university audience that they should kill their parents lends unpleasant support for this sombre world-picture.) The same survey estimates that the 12-25 year-old age-group already totals 700 million and will reach one billion by 1980—a formidable force, indeed.

mercilessly destroyed all vestiges of the older, more cultivated and civilised China. The tragedy is that those slogan-chanting, totally humourless and apparently inhuman young people do not *understand* the cultural values they are destroying, nor do they *understand* the régime they are helping to institute in their place. They are content with action, with the knowledge that they are doing something, and are totally ignorant and heedless of the result of their actions.

Recently student unrest has erupted into mass violence at widely-separated universities: at Berkeley in California and Warsaw in Poland; at the universities of West Berlin, Rome, Paris, Tokyo, London and Wisconsin, among many others. All participants claim to be idealistically motivated, but the curiously similar faces of the student demonstrators, suffused with violence and hatred, scarcely admit the hope that the society they demand would be either as tolerant or as cultured as the one they appear determined to destroy.

Formerly students were assumed to be attending a university in order to learn. Today a growing vociferous minority appears to be there in order to teach; but the permissible and relevant question is surely, how can one teach and advocate radical change unless one first understands the true nature of the problems confronting man and society, problems which have taxed the best minds since the days of Plato and Aristotle? The Red Guard in China and the student demonstrators in Europe and the United States appear to share certain common characteristics: a hatred of anything which commands the allegiance and respect of the older generation, including a contempt for traditional ethical and moral values; a passionate need to be active; and above all a total rejection of authority, both secular and sacred. The folk-heroes of today's youth, Thoreau, Che

135

Guevara, Ho Chi Minh, share one common characteristic with the anti-heroes of Dostoevsky, Osborne, Salinger, *et al*. They were, or are, all in opposition to society which today's activists, as well as artists, regard as hostile, stupid and malignant.

I have already suggested that the true motives of many who participate in apparently idealistic movements may not be so flawlessly altruistic as some observers, and indeed some of the participants themselves, may ingenuously assume. Youth is after all an impulsive rather than a contemplative period and, as Louis Reik observes, 'no high-spirited young man' really wants to face up to the fact 'that the days of unbridled individualism are gone'. As action tends to become an end in itself, causes for dissent and protest are assiduously sought and, when found, become a channel for the natural, aggressive impulses of youth. If, magically, all the reforms and goals which youthful activists are demanding were overnight to become a reality and all their ideals achieved, does anyone seriously believe that this would mean an end to unrest and rebellion?[1]

As the youthful population increases in numbers and power (and it has been estimated that by 1986, 35 per cent of the world's population will be less than 15 years of age), society will come to resemble more and more an automobile with a powerful accelerator and no brakes—a machine which may satisfy youth's craving for speed and danger, but in social terms spells total unrest and eventually the disintegration of civilised life, in short, anarchy. Clearly no society will tolerate such a

---

[1] It may be recalled that John Stuart Mill suffered a nervous breakdown when he realised that he did not wish to see his ideals achieved. They had become such an obsession that he recognised that without their stimulus his life would have been empty and futile.

prospect passively, and the reaction which will take place against the growing youthful rebellion constitutes a great threat to our established political institutions. Democratic societies depend upon the sanctity of law and order, and only where respect for these is almost universal can true democracy survive. The vote and not the street riot, the reasoned argument and not the impassioned demagogic outburst, tolerance and not violent hatred, these are its necessary foundations; but almost wherever one looks today, moderation and restraint appear to be waning amid an excess of largely immature emotionalism.

It has been suggested earlier that there are marked similarities between much of contemporary literature and the literary movement which took place in the latter part of the 18th and the early part of the 19th centuries, that is to say 'romanticism', and if one examines this phenomenon in the light of an ever-growing youthful culture it should cause little surprise. (All the 'romantic' poets died young, including Wordsworth whose poetic life really terminated when he was in his middle thirties.) 'Romanticism' is born essentially of the enthusiasm and rebellion of youth; classicism stems from the wisdom and patience of maturity. Contemporary literature, which in both artistic and economic terms must largely appeal to the young is, in spite of its apparent 'realism', essentially 'romantic'. In fact, the much-vaunted 'realism' is largely confined to the development and exploitation of sex. Homosexuality, lesbianism, castration, rape, transvestism, masturbation—these are held to be the true 'realities' of life, and their 'fearless' display in novels, dramas, and films is regarded as evidence of an adult society treating 'mature' subjects in an honest fashion. Parallel to and coincidental with this is the search for one's 'authentic self', and

137

anything which imposes a curb or a restraint upon such search (self-control, manners, courtesy to others) tends to be regarded as dishonest or hypocritical, the underlying assumption being that the 'authentic self' when found will be essentially primitive and barbaric. This search is but a contemporary version of the 'romantic' cult of 'The Noble Savage', and what we are experiencing in the West today, politically and in terms of literature, is a new form of revolution and 'romanticism', those seemingly inseparable partners. This persistent conjunction becomes intelligible when one realises that both emanate from a desire to escape from things as they are.[1] The 'romantic' writer achieves this escape by means of his artistic imagination, the revolutionary through attempting to translate his vision of a better world into positive action.

To concentrate on sex alone and to imply that it is the sole reality in life, however impeccable in terms of Freudian psychology, is to ignore or exclude large areas of human experience. One only has to consider the comparatively minor role which sex plays in *Macbeth*, *King Lear, Hamlet, Julius Caesar* and *Henry V* or, for that matter, Johnson's *Vanity of Human Wishes* and *Rasselas* (and I suspect that the genuine realism of these last two is too strong for many modern palates), to realise that writers in the past, while not ignoring sex as a potent force in life, were yet aware that mature men

---

[1] Significantly, *Caleb Williams*, a novel by William Godwin (author of the iconoclastic *Enquiry concerning the Principles of Political Justice*) published in 1794, bore the sub-title *Things As They Are*. Godwin, Shelley's somewhat reluctant father-in-law, was in theory at least against the monarchy, aristocracy, property, money, religion and marriage. His life scarcely reflected the high ideals which he professed and he showed a marked financial ability to live off his son-in-law.

and women may have other equally strong drives.[1]

I have already suggested that the contemporary emphasis upon sex and primitivism may be an attempt to impose equality in Freudian rather than Marxist terms. The search for the primitive 'authentic' self is yet another manifestation of this same obsessive, egalitarian cult. If all cultivated arts and accomplishments can be shown to be simply a shallow veneer concealing the animal that lurks beneath the surface, then all men can be reduced to the same lowest common denominator; and that which apparently sets them apart from and above their fellow men—superior intelligence, ability, industry, perseverance and so forth—far from being the virtues they were formerly assumed to be, can be ingeniously represented as hypocritical pretences.

Every revolution must have its myth, and the most persistent of these and the one which, contrary to all human experience, has gained the most 'romantic' adherence over the past century and a half is the belief in the 'equality of man'. As Margaret Mead has written:

'The assumption that men were created equal, with an equal ability to make an effort and win an earthly reward, although denied every day by experience, is maintained every day by our folk-lore and our day dreams'.

In the realm of sport this belief seems curiously absent. No man in his senses would dare to presume that he has, on the grounds of equality, an inalienable right to represent his country in the Olympic games, any more than a boy would imagine he can automatically

[1] This is, basically, the point which Johnson made in his *Preface To Shakespeare* when he wrote:

'But love is only one of many passions; and as it has no great influence upon the sum of life, it has little operation in the dramas of a poet [Shakespeare] who caught his ideas from the living world and exhibited only what he saw before him. He knew that any other passion, as it was regular or exorbitant, was a cause of happiness or calamity'.

claim a place in his school football team. It appears to be widely recognised and accepted that in such activities some are swifter, stronger, more agile than others. Socially and academically, however, the opposite principle is continually asserted and various practical attempts (in the Soviet Union and China, for example) have been made to establish it as a basis for society. All such efforts either have failed or must fail, because no stable society can exist built upon a theory which runs counter to reality. The harsh but unavoidable fact is that men are unequal in terms of hereditary abilities. Some are born with a greater degree of intelligence, a greater capacity for sympathy, a greater ability to succeed than others. Furthermore, even were 'full genitality' to become the universally acknowledged 'final goal of man', one cannot suppress the feeling that in this sphere likewise some would prove 'more equal than others'.

The persistence of this myth and the frustrations which its advocates experience, however, do constitute a grave psychological and political problem. If one were given the wrong solution to a mathematical problem (if one were persuaded, for example, that the answer to five multiplied by three was twenty-five, *had* to be twenty-five), then one would attack the problem repeatedly, attempting to *force* the figures to conform with the erroneous answer. As one repeatedly failed, so one's anger and frustration would mount to frenzy. Many of the proletarian and youthful revolutions which have taken place or are taking place, and which are based upon a similar false assumption, are characterised by a similar frustration and frenzy. One of the *real* problems confronting the world today is how to preserve order, gentleness, compassion and justice while recognising the *inequalities* which exist among men and which will continue to exist while men remain. Even if money, property and all other external indications of superiority were to be abolished, some men (and even more, women) would still appeal to their fellows, whilst others would repel; some would earn the approval of their neighbours, others would forfeit it; some would gain self-respect, others would lose it, and so on. As Samuel Johnson observed:

'So far is it from being true that men are naturally equal, that no two people can be half an hour together but one acquires an evident superiority over the other'.

It is very dubious if this statement can be rationally demolished, but it would be interesting to have the reaction of a 'romantic' egalitarian to it. The doctrine of the 'equality of man' is yet another example of the dangers of abstract thinking divorced from reality.

In economic and artistic terms (and never before have these two become such inseparables), the increasingly youthful market poses an almost insurmountable problem for the mature artist. Never before has society been so permissive; never before has it been so imperative for the artist to be novel, to outshock his competitors, to engage in what Fiedler terms 'the frantic quest for prestige in the pursuit of the chic'. For example, in Alfred Alvarez's *Under Pressure,* a number of distinguished writers stated that their greatest problems were posed by the insatiable public demand for novelty and for technical originality. Coupled with this, the permissiveness of contemporary society was cited as a hindrance rather than a help to the writer, since it removes the stimulus of opposition. 'Without contraries is no progression', wrote Blake and it is possible that complete artistic freedom may prove as much of a bane as other freedoms are found to be when attained.

It would appear that the emergence of artistic move-

141

ments, dominated increasingly by youth, present at least two dangers. The first and most obvious is that they may result in immature artistic standards and goals. As the arts shape society, this will inevitably result in a growing social immaturity; society will grow down rather than up. The consequences, in a world capable of self-extermination, are too obvious to need emphasising. The mature writer, playwright or painter will either have to capitulate, to bow to the standards of the new market-place, or resign himself to catering for a dwindling number who will continue to demand something less jejune in literature, art and painting. The less obvious danger is that, if the young succeed in creating a culture and a society which revolves around those under twenty-five years of age, then they risk spending the greater portion of their lives excluded and isolated from that culture as a succession of youthful cults emerges equally as contemptuous of the previous generation and its goals as today's youth is of traditional culture.

I hope I do not give the impression of being opposed to contemporary youth or fearful of it. What I do fear is power divorced from understanding, power allied to ignorance, power in the hands of secular activists. As an example, a recent French film, *La Chinoise*, portrays a young Maoist student whose consuming ambition is to blow up and totally destroy the Sorbonne. An elderly man (a Marxist and formerly a fighter for Algerian independence) questions her motives. He points out that she is under no compulsion to attend the university and that her plan for its destruction has the support of only a minority of her contemporaries. It transpires in the course of their conversation that there is nothing she wishes to build in place of the Sorbonne and that her real motives are frivolously 'romantic'. She simply

wants to *act* the part of a revolutionary, to ape the life-
style of her heroes and she is not in the least concerned
with the consequences of her actions. (As another
example of juvenile delinquency masquerading as
'revolution' one might cite Abbie Hoffman's *Revolution
For the Hell of It.*)

Clearly, some of the demands which are currently
being made on university authorities throughout the
world are similarly motivated and are aimed less at the
alleged improvement of educational standards than at
the destruction of both the standards and the institutions. Cardinal Newman defined a great intellect as

'one which takes a connected view of old and new, past and
present, far and near, and which has an insight into the
influences of all these one on another'.

Obviously all students cannot be great intellects, but
many are capable of developing an ability to take the
connected view necessary to reach an understanding
of the problems confronting modern man. The contemporary revolutionary mind is hostile to such an
understanding partly because, since all cannot attain it,
it is non-egalitarian. Moreover, a truly educated man is
far too aware of the complexities of life to assume that
there is any *single* or simple solution, whereas the
revolutionary is always convinced that such a solution
exists. In describing the danger, I cannot do better
than quote Burke's words of almost two hundred years
ago in characterising those who conceived and
instigated the French Revolution.

'They have no respect for the wisdom of others, but they pay
it off by a very full measure of confidence in their own. With
them it is a sufficient motive to destroy an old scheme of things
because it is an old one. As to the new, they are in no sort of
fear with regard to the duration of a building run up in haste,
because duration is no object to those who think little or
nothing has been done before their time and who place all
their hopes in discovery. They conceive, very systematically,

that all things which give perpetuity are mischievous, and therefore are at inexpiable war with all establishments.'

This is a most accurate description of what I have referred to throughout this book as temporal provincialism and nothing could be more antithetical to Newman's concept of a great intellect. Since it is the duty and purpose of universities to foster a 'connected view' of human knowledge, they will increasingly become the targets of the contemporary world-wide proletarian and youthful revolutionary movement, a movement which, misquoting Wilde, might be described as the ignorant in full pursuit of ignorance.[1]

A system of higher education which results in mere literacy is a social crime, since it allows its recipients to think they understand the forces shaping world-history when they are only in possession of a number of unrelated and isolated facts. If mass education at university level is worth pursuing, its products must be able to read and *understand* such writers as Spengler, Ortega, and Toynbee. It is not enough for a minority to be acquainted with the nature and extent of the crisis confronting contemporary man. If both the African peasant and the Western university-educated youth are equally ignorant of the awesome spectre of the possible decline and fall of mankind, then there is little hope for the future.

So far I have assumed that writers and other creative artists are free agents, exercising their talents in a volitional manner, and have opposed the alternative assumption because it results in an historical determinism and ultimately an acceptance of total relativism.

[1] It may be recalled that Arnold, aware of the diminishing power of religion, attempted to substitute culture for it, believing that only in this way could anarchy be averted. The contemporary rejection of both religion and culture appears to be producing that anarchical state which Arnold dreaded.

However, Ezra Pound has called the artist 'the antennae of the human race', and Marshall McLuhan defines art as

'a radar which acts as an early alarm system enabling us to discover social and psychic targets in lots of time to prepare to cope with them'.

Both writers imply that the creative artist, because of his greater sensitivity, is more aware than other men of the trends in his contemporary society which will shape the future. The artist is thus regarded as a prophet or seer. If we accept this view, then what future is presaged by contemporary art, saturated as it is with violence and animalism, and with the 'death-oriented hopelessness' which characterises the *avant-garde*? All species which formerly inhabited the earth had a cyclical pattern of youth, maturity, decay and eventual extinction. Does the 'death-oriented hopelessness' signify and forebode not just the decline of Western man but the decline and abolition of mankind?

The problem is more profound than Spengler or Trilling or Fiedler realise, although the titles of their respective books (*The Decline of the West, Beyond Culture, Waiting for the End*) do indicate an awareness of a crisis in life and literature, although they all see it as basically a provincial crisis, applicable only to the West.

I am not of this opinion. Civilisation has, after all, been a heart-breakingly slow process. It has been accomplished through man's gradual realisation that in bodily functions—eating, drinking, copulating, excreting—he differs little from the ape. It was his reasoning ability, his self-control, his 'affectations' which raised him to the dignity of *Homo sapiens*. The contemporary tendency to reject these necessarily repressive concepts may betoken an inevitable, cyclical fall of man. Water-pollution and air-pollution are now quantitatively measurable facts of life, but it also appears that an insidious psychological poison is permeating the modern consciousness, destroying man's mind and moral fibre, leading him back to the primitive jungle from whence he came before that same jungle, devoid of civilised man and trousered ape, returns to its pristine state, the only ultimate victor.

If this is so, then the destructiveness which characterises the work of so many contemporary artists may be seen as a catalytic impulse. If the final result of human history is to be the inevitable decline and fall of the species, then the artist, responding in a vatic or prophetic fashion, with a psychic awareness to this knowledge (apprehended rather than comprehended), will anticipate and even hasten this end. In this respect the artist may be compared to a locomotive. When the train is proceeding *up* a gradient, the locomotive will pull *upwards*. Similarly, when mankind was progressing, the great writers (acting as catalysts) produced works which sustained and elevated men. If we are now experiencing regression, the artist, like a locomotive pulling a train *downhill*, will produce works in which man is induced to despair and in which he is depicted either as a helpless victim or as a passionate and violent creature, devoid of dignity or significance.

Since this result follows from a deterministic attitude, what hope there is arises from a repudiation of such determinism. Man differs from all those species which have previously become extinct in that, through the exercise of conceptual ability, he alone is able to envisage where he stands on the cyclical arc. With this knowledge it is possible for him to take steps to avert his extermination. And this is the challenge confronting all men today, particularly writers, dramatists and other artists. They can either collaborate with the enemy and hasten the destruction of themselves and society, or they can, while not indulging in facile escapism, return to a delineation of an ideal towards which man can strive.

A lack of an understanding of the critical nature of contemporary problems constitutes a major threat to survival. As a society, we are so much better at doing than we are at understanding the consequences of our actions. Our technical ability is unlimited. We can move mountains and make the desert 'blossom as the rose'. We have, in fact, too much technical ability and too much factual knowledge for our culture to absorb and so we are packing knowledge into computers in the hope that they will solve the problems for us. Computers are awesome, impressive objects. They can store millions of facts effortlessly in their 'brains', but they do not *understand* (in human terms) one of the facts which they hoard. There lies their weakness and there also lies man's folly if he abdicates his responsibility and allows them to do his 'thinking' for him.

A world dominated by statistics is a poor substitute for one of understanding, and of the compassion which comes from such an understanding, but occasionally statistics are of assistance in providing an insight into the nature of the contemporary crisis. In the next four years the population of the world will increase by approximately three hundred million (190,000 a day), and this figure takes into account the number of deaths, still-births and so on. In other words, one and a half times as many people as currently inhabit the United States will have been added to the world's population in this short period. Commenting on these figures, Julian Huxley observes that if nothing is done to control this increase,

> 'mankind will drown in its own flood or, if you prefer another metaphor, man will turn into the cancer of the planet'.

147

Recently a play, *Little Murders*, was staged (with only limited success) in New York and London. The action of the play takes place in some undefined future, and the populace is depicted as engaged in random and irrational killings. No one dares to venture out of doors and the city has become a place of siege with mass violence occurring everywhere.[1] I believe that the playwright (Jules Feiffer) is anticipating a very real and horrifying possibility. From an examination of other species in overcrowded conditions we know that such overcrowding results in a form of mass psychosis. Previously docile creatures attack and kill each other, even though still provided with an abundance of food. There is no reason to assume that man is an exception to this phenomenon, and it is surely significant that mass, often irrational, violence almost invariably occurs in the cities where overcrowding and slum conditions conspire to bring about conditions parallel to those observed in the experiments with animals. Man has learned to control death before he has learned to control birth, and far more than most people yet realise we desperately need a sane and cohesive world-population plan. As the economist Kenneth Boulding has stated: 'We are all guilty of ignorance, frivolity and blindness and the accusing fingers of billions of the unborn are pointed angrily towards us'. Arnold Toynbee also makes the following observation on this same problem:

> 'The issue is, indeed, a religious one in the sense that it raises the question, What is the true end of Man? Is it to populate the Earth with the maximum number of human beings . . . or is it to enable human beings to lead the best kind of life that the spiritual limitations of human nature allow?'

Although we have yet to devise an instrument capable

---

[1] One recalls Eliot's view of the future, quoted earlier: 'Internecine fighting . . . People killing one another in the streets.'

of measuring the psychic temperature of a generation or of any particular historical epoch, the spectacle of ever-growing numbers increasingly demanding equal shares in a world where space, food, and consequently the opportunity to live a life of human dignity and significance, are all rapidly diminishing, can only spell total and unrelieved strife and unrest in the years ahead and the children of today's demonstrators may in the 1980s shoulder banners proclaiming the message 'Make *War* Not Love'.

These are the major problems confronting contemporary man. The overwhelming nature and complexity of them may tempt some to seek the quietism of despair, to adopt the hippy creed: 'Tune in, turn on, drop out'. This is not devoid of a certain appeal, but the problems will not disappear if we simply attempt to ignore their existence. Man will prevail (to use Faulkner's words) only if he confronts such problems resolutely and honestly, in a manner best expressed by Tennyson in *Ulysses*:

Though much is taken, much abides and though
We are not now that strength which in old days
Moved heaven and earth, that which we are, we are;
One equal temper of heroic hearts,
Made weak by time and fate, but strong in will
To strive, to seek, to find, and not to yield.

To deny such an ideal, to emphasise man's primitivism, to ignite his baser passions, to question his capacity for sympathy and empathy, in short, to depict him as merely a trousered ape, is not only a form of literary, aesthetic and philosophic dishonesty. It is a sin against life itself, a crime against humanity.

EPILOGUE

This book has grown out of a paper of the same name which was delivered at Jackson's Mill, West Virginia, before a group of university teachers of English in October 1966. On that occasion it created a considerable amount of discussion and controversy lasting well into the night and continuing the following day. Much of the criticism (though by no means all) arose from the fact that, of necessity, a paper-length treatment of the subject omitted a great deal that was germane to the issues involved. This persuaded me that the importance and relevance of the subject demanded a more detailed examination.

Nothing that has happened on the international or domestic scene since I delivered the lecture has changed my opinion that the Western world and its culture are currently saturated with violence and animalism. No one who reads a newspaper or watches a television news programme or who reads an *avant-garde* novel can doubt the truth of this statement, but few seem aware of the underlying causes of this phenomenon. In order to understand the true nature of the chronic upheaval which is engulfing our culture and indeed our entire civilisation, we must look into the past and attempt to trace its genesis there, for the present is simply an outgrowth of what has gone before.

Concluding the Gifford lectures at Edinburgh in 1947, the historian Christopher Dawson declared: 'The recovery of moral control and the return to spiritual order have now become the indispensable conditions of human survival.' The aim of this book has been to re-awaken its readers to a sense of urgency regarding these 'indispensable' conditions. Believing as I do that the arts in general are not merely a mirror reflecting social and cultural values, but are, on the contrary, powerful forces which shape and mould the way in which people live and behave (a view, incidentally, held by every major literary critic from Plato to T. S. Eliot), I have examined contemporary literature, drama, music, painting and those two powerful 'moulders', the cinema and television. In all these various manifestations of the contemporary scene, one finds not only an absence of 'moral control' and 'spiritual order' but in most instances an overt and deep hostility to any such restraining concepts. Morality, however, always involves a sentiment of submission because it demands the recognition of an authoritative norm, be it religious or secular, external (as in former times) or internal (that is, self-imposed). The very terms 'submission' and 'authoritative' appear to be anathemas to an age intoxicated with the concept of 'freedom', but true liberty is surely not so much external as internal; it demands self-control and a punctilious fulfilment of one's obligations.

As Edmund Burke wrote in 1791: 'Men are qualified for civil liberty in exact proportion to their disposition to put moral chains upon their own appetites . . . society cannot exist unless a controlling power upon will and appetite be placed somewhere, and the less of it there is within, the more there is without. It is ordained in the eternal constitution of things that men of intemperate minds cannot be free. Their passions forge their fetters.' No doubt contemporary writers and artists would assert that violence dramatises a situation and that living in a violent world it would be intellectually and socially dishonest to depict life in any other way. If, however, in the novels which he reads, in the plays and films which he sees, and in the philosophical and ethical treatises which are presented for his edification, Western man is continually subjected to a vision of himself as being violent, animalistic, alienated, mannerless and uncivilised, then is he not being encouraged to identify with such an image and to mould his own outlook and behaviour to conform with such an image?

In 1869, Matthew Arnold defined culture as being 'a pursuit of our total perfection by means of getting to know, on all the matters which concern us, the *best* which has been thought and said in the world.' Even the most charitable critic would find it difficult to reconcile Anthony Burgess's *A Clockwork Orange* or a play by Harold Pinter, for example, with this definition and one may be pardoned for assuming that the *worst* that has been thought and said has supplanted the Arnoldian ideal and become the contemporary cultural (or anti-cultural) norm. Lest I be accused of indulging in unsupported generalisations perhaps I ought to provide specific examples even at the risk of appearing to prove what is only too evident. Three representatives and therefore by no means extreme products of the contemporary theatre will perhaps suffice. In Osborne's *A Patriot for Me* two males embrace on the stage; in Picasso's *Le Désir Attrapé par la Queue* a woman, aptly named Tart, squats in a urinating position while a sound track obligingly makes appropriate noises; in Genet's

153

The Balcony a man castrates himself. All three dramatists would doubtless claim that men *do* embrace, that women *do* urinate, that perhaps unbalanced men *do* occasionally castrate themselves. They would also assert that nothing on the contemporary stage can equal in horror the blinding of Gloucester in *King Lear* or the events portrayed in Webster's *The Duchess of Malfi,* to take just two examples.

There are, however, objections to these arguments. Firstly, the blinding of Gloucester is by no means the whole of *Lear,* nor is *Lear* the whole of Shakespeare. There is a balance of light and dark, of hope and despair, of sublimity and degradation in his works—qualities which are absent from much of modern literature. Nor is Webster necessarily the typical voice of that period of English literature. Spenser was also at work on *The Faerie Queene.* Sir Philip Sidney and Francis Bacon were producing respectively the *Arcadia* and the *Novum Organum.* In other words, the best minds of the Elizabethan and Jacobean age produced a dazzling variety of wealth of ideas epitomised perhaps by the magical fusion of passion and intellect which colours all the writings of that remarkable 'man for all seasons', John Donne.

Secondly, over the centuries the cumulative wisdom of society has decreed that if males must embrace they do so in private; urination was also deemed to be a private affair; and presumably if a man must castrate himself then he should do so in the privacy of his own house and not 'frighten the horses.' In other words, the contemporary literary movement while ostensibly bent on 'liberation' is in effect an attack on one of Western man's last and most cherished liberties—the liberty of privacy.

The critic Anthony Lejeune recently asked if anyone really wants 'a society shaped by John Osborne for the delectation of Jimmy Porter, or plunged into lunacy by Harold Pinter or peopled by the hideous imaginings of Genet or Beckett.' He concludes that no one (including these writers) would wish to inhabit such a world. While Lejeune does emphasise the wide gap which exists between the abstract theoretical world presented to the public by these dramatists and the world of reality, he appears to ignore the mania for iconoclasm which permeates the modern arts, an iconoclasm closely linked to egalitarianism. After all, the surest way to achieve complete and absolute equality is to reduce all men to the same level, to deny their dignity, to stress their animalism and to sneer at any form of idealism. Men and women are (superficially, at least) most equal when copulating, masturbating, excreting and urinating, and these are precisely the clinical aspects of human behaviour that the contemporary *avant-garde* has battened on with a zeal formerly associated with the excesses of puritanism.

Indeed, what we are now witnessing both in the arts and in society as a whole is a new form of puritanism and, inverted though it may be, it has the same totalitarian nature allied to a lack of humour and balance which has always characterized puritanism. This 'impuritanism' has taken as part of its Decalogue the following tenets: You *must* not honour your father and mother; you *must* commit adultery (or if not married, fornicate like a ferret); you *must* covet; you *must* steal. All this you *must* do in order to bring about a more just and equal society. In short, 'Do as you're told—revolt!'

155

An ideal is, by definition, a concept or standard of supreme perfection, or in human terms, a person of the highest excellence. Egalitarianism, on the contrary, demands a uniform parity of behaviour and even of attainment. Under these conditions the ideal becomes an enemy; it is regarded no longer as a mode of life to be emulated but as a force to be destroyed, since its existence denies (or at least renders questionable) the whole basis of an egalitarian society.

Contemporary authors, playwrights and poets thus find themselves in a disconcerting dilemma; if they attempt to delineate an ideal, they run the risk of being accused of snobbery, of being anti-proletarian, illiberal, undemocratic and, in certain cases, even racist. Accordingly, all but a dwindling minority have joined the ranks of the iconoclasts, consoling themselves with the thought that they are allied to 'progress'. Ezra Pound sadly expressed this dilemma when he wrote in 'Hugh Selwyn Mauberley':

> The age demanded an image
> Of its accelerated grimace
> Something for the modern stage,
> Not, at any rate, an Attic grace.

Even, for the moment, adopting an egalitarian viewpoint, are we quite certain that *everyone* is mentally and morally prepared for the works of Pinter, Genet, Sartre and Beckett? Have we yet fully taken into account, for example, the social effects not only of television but also of the paperback revolution which, coinciding with new concepts expounded by, and intended for, tough, well-balanced

156

adult minds, brings only too often to an ever-increasing youthful readership a distorted because unbalanced picture of human life and human nature? The question is not so simple as it was in the comparatively elitist society of John Stuart Mill's time. It is no longer simply an either/or between a discontented Socrates and a contented pig. Today one must seriously question the possibility that the net *result* of the contemporary arts may be a society consisting largely of semi-educated, psychologically disturbed human beings. Already countless thousands of the young are demonstrating through drug-reliance and other forms of self-destructive escapism that they have lost what Teilhard de Chardin called 'that essential taste for life'.

Reviewing the English edition of *Trousered Apes* in the *Sunday Telegraph* last year, Peregrine Worsthorne wrote as follows: 'When the Marquis de Sade . . . originally pioneered the artist's exploration of the darker recesses of human depravity, he could at best hope to influence only a tiny fraction of his fellow citizens. His counterparts today, however, thanks to mass literacy and mass communications, can and do speak to all, their messages of corruption enjoying an ease of instant dissemination, an absence of contradiction and the certainty of vulgarisation that immediately transform them from a minority cult to a mass craving. . . . Of course the artist must be allowed to drive himself mad. But must he be allowed to drive us all mad?'

To those who may object that certain passages in this book are 'reactionary', I would simply suggest that if one saw a blind man tottering precariously on the edge of a cliff, one's instinctive reaction would be to counsel him to remain immobile and then to take a step backwards. Western society, blinded by its technological sophistication and neglectful of the things of the spirit, resembles in many ways just such a situation. If it proceeds on its present course —a course which has produced a society recently described as one consisting of technological giants and moral pygmies—then the seemingly inevitable end will be the extermination of the species, probably with a whimper rather than a bang. Man does, however, differ from other creatures which have become extinct in that he possesses the conceptual ability (if he will only exercise it) to realise where he stands in relation to his past and to his problematical future.

What we are in danger of forgetting, however, is that no valid discussion of such a hypothetical future can, in the last analysis, ignore the question of human *value*. If a man is induced to regard himself as *merely* a trousered ape, or 'a walking bag of sea water' as certain scientists choose to see him, or a complex but predictable collection of reactions to various stimuli as Dr. B. F. Skinner and other behaviourists assert, then he is simply an exceptionally extravagant, predatory and messy mammal, and apart from a natural but sentimental loyalty to one's own species his disappearance from the scene would ecologically be no disaster.

However, as Joseph Wood Krutch has pointed out: 'Man's arts, his religion and his civilisation—these are fair and wonderful things but they are fair and wonderful to him alone. With the extinction of his poetry would be extinguished also the only sensibility for which it has any meaning and there would remain nothing capable of feeling a loss'.

Great literature is that which over the centuries *sustained* and *elevated* mankind; it represents a conquest by man over the diverse and bewildering complexities of his own nature and of the world surrounding him. Such art involves a prodigious effort and concentration on the part of its creator and demands a cultivated response from its audience. As such it is exclusive, in terms of those who create it and those who can appreciate it. It therefore constitutes a minority culture and is to be detested and feared by the majority of contemporary artists and writers with their egalitarian aims and allegiance, reinforced by the financial rewards of catering to an undiscriminating mass market.

However, if much of contemporary literature no longer supports the human spirit, if on the contrary it spreads despair, alienation, emptiness and spiritual sterility, then it should be challenged since it is contrary to the survival of the species. Man *is* more than a physical animal. He needs, above all, *hope* to endure. The destruction of such hope and the dissemination of nihilism appear to be the message of the new impuritanism, which is not simply the old puritanism 'writ large' but which springs from a barely concealed cultural, social and individual death-wish.

In view of the urgency of the present cultural crisis, my aim has been to reach as wide a public as possible and, for this reason, I have tried to write for the educated general reader and not the specialist. I must ask the latter's indulgence for many passages which have, no doubt, to him seemed either oversimplified or even elementary.

Finally, I must acknowledge the kindness of Malcolm Muggeridge who not only has supplied the eloquent Foreword to this book but has done so much to help and sustain me in all my work. No one could have had a more constant or generous friend.

SELECTED BIBLIOGRAPHY

Arnold, Matthew, *Culture and Anarchy*, John Murray, London, 1962.

Barzun, Jacques, *The House of Intellect*, Secker & Warburg, London, 1962.

Bate, Walter Jackson, *From Classic to Romantic*, Harper & Row, New York, 1961.

Booth, Wayne, *The Rhetoric of Fiction*, University of Chicago Press, Chicago, 1961.

Boulding, Kenneth, *The Meaning of the Twentieth Century*, Allen & Unwin, London, 1964.

Brinton, Crane, *The Anatomy of Revolution*, Jonathan Cape, London, 1953.

Burke, Edmund, *Reflections on the Revolution in France*, ed. C. C. O'Brien, Penguin Books, Harmondsworth, 1969.

———— 'Thoughts on French Affairs', in *Three Memorials on French Affairs*, London, 1797.

Camus, Albert, *Resistance, Rebellion and Death*, Hamish Hamilton, London, 1964.

———— *The Myth of Sisyphus*, Hamish Hamilton, London, 1955.

———— *The Rebel*, Penguin Books, Harmondsworth, 1969.

Cary, Joyce, *Charley Is My Darling*, Pergamon Press, 1968.

Cecil, Lord David, *Poets and Story-Tellers*, Constable, London, 1970.

Cowley, Malcolm (ed.), *After the Genteel Tradition*, P. Smith, Carbondale, U.S., 1959.

Cruikshank, John, *Albert Camus*, Oxford University Press, London, 1960.

Dawson, Christopher, *Religion and Culture: The Gifford Lectures 1947*, New York, 1965.

Dostoevsky, Fyodor, *Crime and Punishment*, trans. Constance Garnett, New York, 1951; trans. David Magarshack, Penguin Books, Harmondsworth, 1970.

———— *Notes From Underground,* trans. Ralph E. Matlaw, Bradda Books, New York, 1962.

Eliot, T. S., 'Religion and Literature', in *Essays Ancient and Modern by T. S. Eliot,* New York, 1936.

———— *Thoughts After Lambeth,* London, 1931.

Fiedler, Leslie A., *Waiting for the End,* Penguin Books, Harmondsworth, 1967.

Fletcher, Joseph, *Situation Ethics: The New Morality,* Student Christian Movement Press, London, 1967.

Fromm, Erich, *Escape From Freedom,* Holt, London, 1941.

Frye, Northrop, *The Modern Century,* Oxford University Press, London, 1969.

Golding, William, *Lord of the Flies,* Faber & Faber, London, 1954.

Huxley, Aldous, *The Politics of Ecology: The Question of Survival,* Center for the Study of Democratic Institutions, Santa Barbara, California, 1963.

Huxley, Julian, 'World Population', in *Scientific American,* March 1956.

Jarry, Alfred, *Ubu Roi,* trans. Barbara Wright, in *Four Modern French Comedies,* New York, 1960; Gaberbocchus Press, London, 1966.

Johnson, Pamela Hansford, *On Inquiry,* Macmillan, London, 1967.

Katope, Christopher G., and Zolbrod, Paul G. (eds.), *Beyond Berkeley,* Cleveland, 1966.

Kluckhohn, Clyde, 'Values and Value-Orientation in the Theory of Action', in *Towards a General Theory of Action,* ed. Talcott Parsons and Edward A. Shils, Cambridge, Mass., 1951.

Krutch, Joseph Wood, *The Modern Temper,* New York, 1929.

Leavis, F. R., *Revaluation,* Peregrine Books, London, 1964.

Lewis, C. S., *The Abolition of Man,* Geoffrey Bles, London, 1946.

Lovejoy, Arthur O., *The Great Chain of Being,* Harper & Row, New York, 1960.

McLuhan, Marshall, *Understanding Media: The Extensions of Man,* Sphere Books, London, 1970.

McNeill, William H., *The Rise of the West,* University of Chicago Press, Chicago, 1968.

Mumford, Lewis, The City in History, Penguin Books, Harmondsworth, 1966.

Newman, John Henry, The Idea of a University, ed. Svaglic, Holt, Rinehart & Winston, London, 1960.

Ortega y Gasset, J., The Dehumanisation of Art, Princeton University Press, Princeton, N.J., 1969.

———— The Modern Theme, Harper & Row, New York, 1961.

———— The Revolt of the Masses, Allen & Unwin, London, 1951.

Orwell, George, Animal Farm, Secker & Warburg, London, 1945.

Osborne, John, Look Back in Anger, Faber & Faber, London, 1957.

Pope, Alexander, 'An Essay On Man', in The Poems of Alexander Pope, ed. John Butt, New Haven, 1963.

Richards, I. A., Science and Poetry, London, 1926.

Robinson, John A. T., Honest To God, Student Christian Movement Press, London, 1963.

Santayana, George, The Genteel Tradition at Bay, New York, 1931.

Shelley, Percy Bysshe, Prometheus Unbound, A Variorum Edition, ed. Lawrence J. Zillman, Seattle, 1959; Heath, London, 1892.

Sorokin, Pitirim A., The Crisis of Our Age, New York, 1943.

Spengler, Oswald, The Decline of the West, trans. Charles Francis Atkinson 2 vols., Allen & Unwin, London, 1961.

Teilhard de Chardin, P., The Phenomenon of Man, trans. Bernard Wall, New York, 1965.

Tocqueville, Alexis de, Democracy in America, trans. G. Lawrence, Fontana, London, 1968.

Toynbee, Arnold J., A Study of History, 10 vols., Oxford University Press, London, 1960.

Trilling, Lionel, Beyond Culture, Penguin Books, Harmondsworth, 1967.

———— The Liberal Imagination, New York, 1953.

Wellwarth, George, The Theater of Protest and Paradox, New York, 1964.

Wertham, Fredric, A Sign For Cain, Robert Hale, London, 1968.

Williams, Kathleen, Jonathan Swift and the Age of Compromise, Kansas University Press, Kansas, 1968.

Winters, Yvor, In Defense of Reason, Routledge & Kegan Paul, London, 1960.